2/11

EXTREME SURVIVAL

Extreme Survival

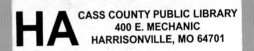

For Bella and Luca

Let the adventure begin

ACKNOWLEDGMENTS

I am hugely indebted to a great number of people whose professionalism has ensured both the safety and success of the Serious Adventure series. They have provided invaluable insights into the setting up and smooth running of extreme expeditions, many of which are reflected in this book.

In particular, expedition leader Bruce Parry blazed the trail heading up both Serious Jungle and Serious Desert, coolly taking twelve- to fifteen-year-olds to new horizons under the round-the-clock scrutiny of the TV cameras. Bruce also kindly wrote the foreword to the book.

The expeditions company Trekforce provided logistics and safety for the original Serious Jungle expedition under MD Rob Murray John, and their great experience and expedition philosophy has informed all subsequent series.

Enormous thanks are also due to current expedition leader Ben Major plus expedition medics Dr. Stephan Sanders and Dr. Antonia Lile who have generously shared their knowledge and checked the information contained in this book—though of course responsibility for the accuracy of all the contents remains completely mine.

Among the many others whose expertise in extreme environments has also contributed to the series are assistant leaders Emma Jay and Polly Murray; expedition coordinators Dougie Warner, Phil Ashby, Huan Davies, Michael Robinson, Greg Coe, and Matt Leggett; local experts and charity partners Matty McNair, Christian Zdanowicz, Roxanne Kremer, Blythe Loutit, Mike Hearn, Fernando Cobo, Armando Castillanos, Compania de Guias de Montaña, and the many local guides and rangers whose know-how has been absolutely priceless. Apologies to all those I have not been able to mention by name.

Back at base at BBC TV, I would like to thank my executive producer Reem Nouss for her wisdom and support over so many years in negotiating the editorial and safety minefield, Angela Wallis and the BBC New Talent team for their continued backing from the very start, and Nigel Pickard for showing the vision and faith to commission the series in the first place.

At HarperCollins it has been an absolute pleasure to work with Myles Archibald, Julia Koppitz, Jilly Macleod, and designer Nicola Croft.

Finally, a few special thanks: to all the young adventurers whose bravery, dedication and spirit of adventure have been an extraordinary example of what young people are capable of achieving; to their parents who not only brought up such talented children but trusted us to look after them in such extreme environments; and to my partner Jenny who hunted down expedition jargon in the book, and has been left so often holding our twins, born the week the series was first commissioned, as I've constantly disappeared to some of the world's remotest parts.

Marshall Corwin, Series Producer/Director, Serious Adventure

Skyhorse Publishing books may be purchased in bulk at special discounts for sales promotion, corporate gifts, fund-raising, or educational purposes. Special editions can also be created to specifications. For details, contact the Special Sales Department, Skyhorse Publishing, 555 Eighth Avenue, Suite 903, New York, NY 10018 or info@skyhorsepublishing.com.

www.skyhorsepublishing.com

10 9 8 7 6 5 4 3 2 1

Library of Congress Cataloging-in-Publication Data

Corwin, Marshall.
  Extreme survival / Marshall Corwin.
    p. cm.
  ISBN 978-1-61608-000-6 (hardcover : alk. paper)
  1. Wilderness survival. 2. Survival skills. I. Title.
  GV200.5.C67 2010
  613.6'9--dc22

                                      2009047158

This book was originally published by HarperCollins UK under the title, *Serious Survival*.

Printed in China

CONTENTS

Foreword

In our modern culture we no longer have a formal rite of passage for young people into adulthood. No way for them to prove themselves to their peers and elders. We have fewer physical challenges for them to complete. We make their lives easier in many ways. We sterilize their environment, wrap them in health and safety bandages and are paranoid about them ever being alone. To me this is a shame.

I have rarely been so impressed with a group of people as I have with the two teams of kids that I took away on the first two Serious expeditions. I also know that my great friend Ben Major, who has led every Serious trip since, feels similarly. In both of my expeditions I put the groups of young people into situations that would have made most adults balk. Yes, we had some tears—plenty at times—and we had numerous problems which often seemed insurmountable, but in every case the young teams overcame immense difficulties and came out the other side shining.

Expeditions aren't so much about learning new skills and processes, but more about learning about yourself and those around you in your team. A great way to do that is to be placed into a situation you've never dealt with before. On the Serious adventures, each expedition member pushed their physical and mental boundaries far beyond what they had ever considered possible. They all found some extra reserve of strength, stamina and fortitude that they never knew they had. And of course, the beauty is that they now know that

extra something is there, residing within them, if they ever need it again. They've all been given a great gift.

When all their friends run for cover on the station platform because the storm comes in, they can stand it out if they so desire, because they know it's only rain and nothing could be as bad as the week of solid rain in the jungle when they had to look after themselves, try and light a fire, cook, trek through muddy paths and streams, and more, just to go to work for the day. A better understanding of their personal comfort threshold in youth has awarded them a lifetime of self-confidence.

To my mind we are all capable of such achievement. It's known that even the least likely of characters, in a survival situation, can be capable of great feats of bravery, physical prowess, and mental agility. This book reflects the philosophy of the series, namely that expeditions can be for everyone. Not just the realm of specialist climbers, macho explorers. I applaud all those great young people who took part in the Serious expeditions. They have inspired innumerable adults and children to get out there and push themselves in some way. I hope this book inspires you to do the same.

Bruce Parry
Ibiza 2007

Bruce in the Namib during the filming of Serious Desert. He also led the very first Serious expedition to the Borneo jungle.

Preparing for the Wild

SERIOUS ADVENTURE

Adventure has always been central to the human spirit. Throughout history people have bravely headed into uncharted territory in search of new horizons; sometimes simply finding food and shelter has meant a battle of wits against all the natural world has to offer. But as our standard of living soars beyond the wildest dreams of our ancestors we are gradually losing touch with our adventurous side—and we're all the poorer for it.

For the past five years the BBC TV Serious Adventure series has tried to redress the balance, taking teams of young adventurers to some of the most hostile and remote environments on earth. The twelve- to fifteen-year-olds have quite literally gone to extremes to help the planet—not only coping with conditions that would challenge many an adult explorer, but also completing major environmental projects to benefit key endangered species such as orangutans and polar bears.

For the participants, the expeditions have been life-changing, opening their eyes to a whole new world way beyond their day-to-day experiences back home. The trips have also demonstrated that with the right preparations and attitude, most people are capable of achieving far more than they might first think.

ALL IN THE MIND

It can't be emphasised enough that the key to heading outside your "comfort zone" into harsh environments is mental attitude. Yes, basic fitness is important, preparation is fundamental, and expert assistance is often vital, but time and again a "can-do" positive outlook has been proven to make all the difference in the world.

It's not about revelling in being uncomfortable, dirty and tired—most adventurers love their luxury hotel just like the next person. It's the deep satisfaction of pushing yourself to new limits and experiencing all that life has to offer.

And at the end of a tough expedition you'll appreciate that five star hotel all the more—even if the hotel receptionists show slightly less appreciation of the filthy, bedraggled individuals lowering the tone of their lobby.

FITNESS

A basic level of fitness is essential for most expeditions—walking any distance with a backpack at altitude or in the heat of a jungle is debilitating at the best of times, and is certainly no fun if you're really unfit. Plan an exercise program that gradually increases in intensity (and if you're not used to exercise, talk through your proposed program with your doctor or a fitness expert).

For stamina, half-hour walks and short jogs at least three times a week should build to longer hikes of several hours as you get closer to the trip. Carry a backpack and use the boots you'll be using on the expedition to wear them in. Regular gym sessions will also improve your strength.

Having said that, it's important to keep things in perspective and not become obsessed—only the most extreme challenges, such as attempting a Himalayan peak or walking to the North or South Pole, require superhuman fitness.

Once on location experiencing the outdoor life, your stamina will increase further day by day. With luck you'll be absolutely glowing with health by the time you return.

ADVENTURE WITH A PURPOSE

All Serious Adventure trips have an environmental goal, and you might want to look at whether you can also add this extra dimension to your trip. It can be extremely satisfying knowing you are helping the environment, and it may also help you through any difficult times when tough conditions threaten to get the better of you.

Many trekking and expedition companies offer such opportunities, and various animal groups are on the lookout for volunteers to help with projects in the field. Even if you don't take part formally, they may be interested in information gathered about sightings of endangered creatures.

Everything you do on expedition should of course be planned with the maximum respect—and minimum disturbance—for the environment, animals, and local people. As the old maxim says: Take nothing but photographs, leave nothing but footprints.

PROTECTION AGAINST DISEASE

a) Inoculations

Most extreme locations require a range of inoculations to protect against diseases such as typhoid, yellow fever, and hepatitis A and B (to name but a few). Your doctor or a travel clinic will be able to advise as to what is needed for the particular area you intend to visit. Get onto this early as some diseases need a course of inoculations over a period of a month or more before departure.

The inoculations required will also depend on the immunizations you were given as a young child and whether these are still "in date."

b) Malaria tablets

Many locations need protection against malaria. Anti-malaria drugs are usually taken as a course of tablets beginning before the expedition and continuing until well after the trip has ended. The exact drugs recommended will depend on the type of malaria found in the area visited (see also Staying Healthy, page 92).

Safety

It's always hard to assess the true risk of an expedition in an extreme environment. As you start to list the potential hazards, the trip can quickly begin to look like a complete nightmare that nobody in their right mind should undertake. The trick is highlighting the dangers without overplaying the risks. (It's often said, with some statistical justification, that the most dangerous parts of an extreme expedition are actually the journeys to and from the airport.)

A way to get the risks in perspective is to imagine how dangerous, say, remote Amazon tribespeople would find our day-to-day life in "civilization." Never having seen traffic before their chances of safely crossing a busy road would be extremely low.

To ensure survival they would clearly need to key into advice and expertise from local people, which is exactly what anyone planning a trip to their environment should also be doing.

MANAGING RISK

Everything is risky. For example, many people break their leg before even leaving the house by tripping over the doorstep. The aim during an expedition is to reduce the risks to an acceptably low level. There are various things to help achieve this:

- Careful planning in advance of the trip is essential, taking into account all the worst case scenarios and the actions that will be taken should the worst actually happen.
- Critical to this "risk assessment" is an evacuation plan, listing how you would get someone to a suitably equipped, first-class hospital at any point on the expedition and how long it would take. If in the territory of dangerous snakes, for example, you will generally need to ensure that you are no more than four hours from a hospital with anti-venom.
- Local expert guides are indispensable.
- Fully charged satellite phones should be carried by key members of the expedition at all times, along with GPS satellite handsets to pinpoint location. Don't forget spare batteries.
- A number of two way VHF radios (walkie talkies) may greatly help communication between key expedition members.
- If going to very remote areas consider taking an EPIRB (Emergency Position-Indicating Radio Beacon), which will transmit your position to the rescue services in case of dire emergency.

Safety training exercises during the Serious Amazon expedition

- Employ the buddy system, in which expedition members are paired up for the duration of the trip. The aim is that each looks out for the other at all times: they should always know where their "buddy" is to ensure they don't get lost. The pair should regularly inspect each other to check for frostbite, leeches, rashes, and so on.
- Each member of the expedition should carry their emergency kit at all times (see Essential Gear, page 14).
- A medic should ideally accompany the expedition with a full emergency medical kit to stabilize casualties. If this is not possible, ensure that at least one member of the party is trained in first aid, and bring a medical kit appropriate to the region as advised by a good travel clinic.
- Take out full medical and evacuation insurance to cover local hospital treatment and repatriation.
- Check out travel advice for the country you are traveling to on the U.S. Department of State website www.travel.state.gov.

EMERGENCY NUMBERS

Fill in this checklist (where relevant) before you go, to make sure you have all the necessary numbers in case of an emergency.

Nearest embassy or consulate

Local helicopter/plane evacuation

Insurance company for evacuation/medical emergency

Local hospital

Emergency mobile

Telemedicine service

Expedition satellite phones

Local charity partner

Emergency contacts

EPIRB (Emergency Position-Indicating Radio Beacon)

IN AN EMERGENCY

Before going on a trip, make your own emergency card reminding you of what to do should anything go wrong. The Serious Expedition team emergency card reads as follows:

Lost or Separated?
DON'T PANIC
CONSERVE/RATION WATER & FOOD
    S.O.S. Signal (noise or light):
    3 short + 3 long + 3 short
    OR 6 blasts/bangs/light per minute
    (Reply—3 blasts)
DO NOT MOVE LOCATION
WE WILL FIND YOU
STAY COOL
STAY POSITIVE

–?–HOW DO YOU avoid jet lag traveling across the world?

Jet lag is caused by traveling across time zones, which messes up your internal body clock, disrupts sleep patterns, and leaves you exhausted. It can't be avoided and its effects are exacerbated by arrival in a hot, humid environment, so it's wise to do all you can to minimize the effects.

At the start of the journey it often helps to set your watch to the local time at your destination and eat and sleep accordingly. Even if you can't actually sleep on a plane, cat naps will pay dividends.

Don't go charging off on expedition the moment you arrive. If possible allow several very light days on arrival to recover from jet lag and to acclimate.

TRAVEL TIPS

- Long plane journeys leave you dehydrated. Drink lots of water, avoid alcohol, and get up regularly and walk around the cabin.
- The journey from the airport is potentially one of the most dangerous things you'll do all trip. Invest in reliable, safe transport from the airport with a reputable company (colorful local forms of transport such as three-wheeler motorbike taxis can be death-traps).
- As soon as you arrive in a tropical country, drink only purified water. That means avoiding drinking or brushing your teeth with tapwater, and being meticulous about not eating anything that may have been washed in tapwater, for example delicious-looking salads. Particularly tempting in a hot environment is to have ice cubes in your drinks, but sadly you should refuse unless you know for sure that the ice has been made from filtered water.
- Always clean your hands before eating, using alcohol gel rather than the local water.
- Don't eat any food, especially meat, unless you are sure it has just been cooked. Give the mouthwatering platter of cold meats a miss—how long has it been sitting there?
- Don't automatically trust the global hotel chains. Their hygiene standards may be woefully short of their counterparts in more developed countries. Many is the time folk have successfully completed the most extreme trip, only to get food poisoning at the last minute after celebrating with a blowout at a "luxury" hotel before their flight out.
- Do your research into local customs. For example, will taking photos of local people offend them? Learning a few basic words such as "hello" and "thank you" in the local language will go a long way.
- Work out a secure way of carrying your money, tickets, and passport, such as a waist belt which fastens securely and can be hidden beneath loose clothing.
- Keep a photocopy of your key passport pages separate to your passport, along with numbers for your nearest embassy or consulate in case of emergency.

Essential Gear

Carrying on your back all you need to live in an extreme environment can give you an enormous sense of freedom, but it can also be quite a pain for a number of reasons:

- What seems manageable for a few minutes back home may feel pretty intolerable after six hours of trekking up and down slippery slopes in humid, dense jungle.
- Getting the amount of gear down to an acceptable weight may be an almighty struggle.
- The item you desperately need always seems to end up at the bottom of the backpack, requiring everything to come out (usually in torrential rain).

WHAT SHOULD I TAKE WITH ME ON EXPEDITION?

There are of course some absolute essentials, but the principle is to take as little as possible. Constantly remind yourself that anything that goes with you will almost certainly have to be carried on your back in a backpack in extreme conditions— and on most expeditions you will also have to make room for group gear, such as food and pots and pans.

Your actual gear list will depend on where you're going (see appropriate chapters for details) and on personal preference. People get very attached to particular items of gear. But a few basic principles apply:

- You generally need far fewer changes of clothes than you imagine. It is not at all unusual to

manage for weeks on expedition with just a couple of sets of clothes and around three sets of underwear.
- Most personal toiletries are a complete waste of space and time. Take advice before taking hair products, creams, and deodorant to, say, an environment where you'll be dripping with sweat and covered in mud all day. Once you've decided what is really essential, transfer the minimum amount to small plastic bottles to save weight. Replace bulky spray cans with more compact products. For example, ditch the shaving cream and use a tiny bottle of shaving oil.
- Draw up a checklist well in advance of departure to ensure you have all essentials. Then treat them with extreme care—your life may depend on it (and replacing invaluable items once on expedition is often impossible).

EMERGENCY KIT

When traveling in an extreme environment there are various essentials you must keep with you at all times in case of emergency—primarily if lost or split off from the group.

Where you keep the kit will depend on the environment, but it should never leave your side except when safely inside camp.

In the jungle or desert, many like the flexibility of the military solution—the belt kit with a series of pouches slung round the waist. (This can, however, interfere with the positioning of your backpack waist strap and is completely impractical if also wearing a climbing harness.)

The exact contents of an emergency kit are always the subject of debate, but as a general guide they may include the following:

- water
- whistle
- compass
- waterproof matches, candle, and fire-lighting tinder such as cotton balls
- iodine drops to purify water and to sterilize wounds
- emergency snack, such as a high-energy cereal bar
- pocketknife
- small torch plus spare batteries
- sunblock
- mosquito/insect repellent and malaria tablets (if required)
- a few sheets of toilet roll
- several yards of parachute cord (strong string)
- personal medical kit including pain killers, plasters, and rehydration salts
- emergency card

In a humid or potentially wet environment, the emergency kit should be packed in zip-up plastic bags, such as freezer bags.

PACKING BACKPACKS

Packing your backpack is quite an art. It's not just about getting everything in, though that may be tricky enough. The load has to be balanced so it's comfortable to wear, and you need to be able to reach essentials in a hurry. For most expeditions it all has to be waterproofed to withstand torrential downpours—and even possibly immersion in a river.

For waterproofing the principle is: "In a bag, in a bag, in a bag." In other words, three layers consisting of a) smaller waterproof bags called stuff sacs, which go in b) a large waterproof backpack liner, which goes in c) the backpack itself. Not only will this arrangement keep the contents dry, it will also help you organize your gear as you can use separate stuff sacs for different sorts of items. You should put items you'll need in a hurry in the stuff sacs nearest the top of your backpack.

Any particularly heavy items should also go near the top to keep you balanced when trekking. Take expert advice on adjusting straps. Many modern backpacks can be fitted to your body size to help distribute the weight comfortably, but you can spend many an uncomfortable hour trying to sort it out by trial and error.

If you'll be spending several days based at the same camp, you may also want to take a much smaller backpack with you for use when going out for the day.

Serious

◇ THE POLAR REGIONS

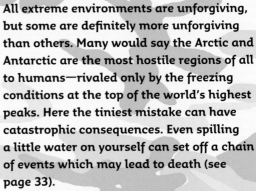

All extreme environments are unforgiving, but some are definitely more unforgiving than others. Many would say the Arctic and Antarctic are the most hostile regions of all to humans—rivaled only by the freezing conditions at the top of the world's highest peaks. Here the tiniest mistake can have catastrophic consequences. Even spilling a little water on yourself can set off a chain of events which may lead to death (see page 33).

Imagine living inside a freezer for weeks on end, then think way, way colder and you start to get some idea of typical polar conditions (average freezer: −18°C/−0.4°F; average Arctic winter's day: −30°C/−22°F).

On first arrival in the region, many adventurers suffer "Arctic shock," a state of near

Arctic

panic where their body urgently tells them it doesn't appreciate such crazy temperatures. All they can think of is getting back into the warmth as quickly as possible.

The secret is to adopt a completely different mindset. Everything has to be adjusted to the fact that you're boldly going where humans were never designed to be (apart from the native peoples— see Inuit Survival, page 60). Things that take a few seconds back in "civilization," such as getting into bed, may well need a good half hour in the freezing conditions.

The rewards are great, and not just the huge satisfaction of joining an elite band who've "been there, done that" and lived to tell the tale. The Arctic and Antarctic are breathtakingly beautiful. Whether it's the extraordinary ice sculptures formed by the wind and the sea, or the spectacular Northern and Southern Lights, the polar regions have an unearthly, almost spiritual appeal.

TO THE ENDS OF THE EARTH

The first explorers to take on the North and South Poles were phenomenal pioneers, heading into some of the harshest conditions on Earth without any of the safety nets modern adventurers take for granted, such as GPS satellite navigation devices and satellite phones to call in assistance.

The famous race for the South Pole in 1911 saw the Norwegian team headed by Roald Amundsen triumph over their British rivals led by Captain Robert Scott. The British team did reach the Pole just over a month after the Norwegians, but tragically all died on their return journey.

Robert Peary is often credited as being the first to get to the North Pole, in 1909, but this is disputed. An American team made it in 1968, using snowmobiles, while the first confirmed non-

ARCTIC V ANTARCTIC

The two polar regions on the planet have much in common. They do, however, have some significant differences (see below).

ARCTIC	ANTARCTIC
Made up of the Arctic Ocean (much of it frozen) surrounded by the northernmost parts of several countries including the USA (Alaska), Canada, Greenland, Norway, and Russia.	A huge continent covered in ice. No country owns Antarctica.
The North Pole is located in an area of frozen sea ice that constantly drifts and breaks up. Adventurers find it hard to stay precisely at the Pole as the ice sheets shift beneath their feet.	The South Pole is located pretty well in the middle of the Antarctic land mass, at an altitude of almost 3,000 m (10,000 ft). A ceremonial pole and flag has been planted at the South Pole and there is a permanent scientific research station nearby.
Inhabited sparsely by indigenous peoples.	Has no native peoples.
The kingdom of the polar bear, plus other mammals including caribou and foxes. (But absolutely no penguins!)	The kingdom of the penguin. Has no land-based mammals at all.

THE LAND OF THE MIDNIGHT SUN

The Arctic Circle is a special line of latitude at around 66°N. It marks the furthest distance from the North Pole where each year you get at least one full 24-hour day when the sun doesn't set, and one full day of complete darkness. As you get nearer to the Pole there are more and more summer days when the sun doesn't set, and more winter days when the sun never rises. At the Pole itself you get six months of daylight followed by six months of darkness.

The same properties apply to the Antarctic Circle at 66°S, though with the seasons reversed.

THE NORTHERN AND SOUTHERN LIGHTS

Also known as the Aurora Borealis and Aurora Australis, the Northern and Southern Lights are shimmering, ever-changing curtains of light in the night sky, caused by radiation from the sun hitting the Earth's magnetic field near the Poles.

The Serious Arctic Adventure

Like most Arctic adventurers, the Serious Arctic team mounted their expedition at the start of spring. The aim was to hit a narrow weather window (usually late March to early May), avoiding the almost constant darkness and impossibly cold conditions of mid-winter, but arriving before the sea ice began to break up too badly.

Stepping off the plane was quite a shock. The team were "lucky" to fly in on a relatively mild spring day, but with the temperature at −18°C (0.4°F) it was still like walking into a freezer. One young adventurer commented that the air froze inside her nose and it felt like she'd got concrete up it.

They were immediately whisked out onto the frozen sea on snowmobiles for a week of acclimation and Arctic training. Until their return to civilization, they would now constantly live, eat, and sleep in a frozen world. Their training camp, a spartan, corrugated-iron Nissen hut erected on the sea ice in the middle of Frobisher Bay, was quite surreal. Like the main expedition tents, the temperature inside would rarely rise above zero. It meant almost everything taken for granted in normal life had to be rethought, a lesson quickly learnt by the adventurers. Having taken out bars of chocolate for a snack, they nearly broke their teeth—the chocolate was frozen solid.

The expedition had two environmental missions: to help gather data for a polar bear research project and to take measurements of a glacier as part of research into global warming. Polar bears live and hunt where the sea ice meets the open ocean, which meant a marathon journey by husky sled down Frobisher Bay. Everything the expedition team needed for two weeks living rough had to be carried on just four sleds. To avoid treacherous areas where the sea ice was too thin, the team ducked inland over spectacular frozen

This image was seen on billboards around the UK to promote Serious Arctic.

The young adventurers take some rare time out (right).

lakes. The wind had whipped up reducing the temperature to around –30°C (–22°F), but as memories of warmth and running water faded, the young adventurers finally began to adapt and cope with the extreme conditions.

Unfortunately, hostile environments have a habit of keeping you on your toes. An unexpected, ferocious storm ripped through the camp in the middle of the night with winds of up to 100 miles an hour. Tents that had survived the North and South Poles were torn to shreds, but the expedition's emergency planning held up. The adventurers were quickly transferred to smaller dome tents that had survived the assault. Nobody was injured, though some of the team were seriously freaked out by the experience.

At the end of a truly epic journey, covering 160 km (100 miles) in five days, they headed back down into Frobisher Bay at the edge of the frozen ocean. The team were at last in polar bear territory, and were looking forward hugely to seeing the majestic creatures at last. But once again the unpredictable Arctic struck. For three days they were storm-bound in unseasonably bad weather as blizzards reduced visibility to almost zero. The leaders were forced to abandon the polar bear

phase completely to keep the expedition on schedule, a salutary lesson in the day-to-day difficulties faced by animal researchers.

The fourth day spent camped on the sea ice saw perfect blue skies once more, and the adventurers were treated to an awesome journey by snowplane onto the Grinnell Glacier. Just a handful of researchers had ever visited the glacier—more people have walked on the Moon. If it had been cold at sea level, this was a whole new level of bone-chilling misery. They were almost 1,000 m (3,000 ft) up and with constant strong winds the temperature plummeted to –40°C (–40°F).

Energy reserves were at a low after two weeks of living on the frozen land, making the survey work almost unbearably tough. News that another storm was on the way, delaying their departure off the glacier, was the last thing they wanted to hear. They could do nothing but sit it out in their tents, which is pretty routine for glaciologists who plan for extended periods waiting for a window in the weather. The young adventurers had a relatively short wait of just two days, but when the snowplane finally made it through to whisk them back to civilization it was a sight they would never forget.

The Twin Otter snowplane lands on its skis on the sea ice.

EXPEDITION LOCATION

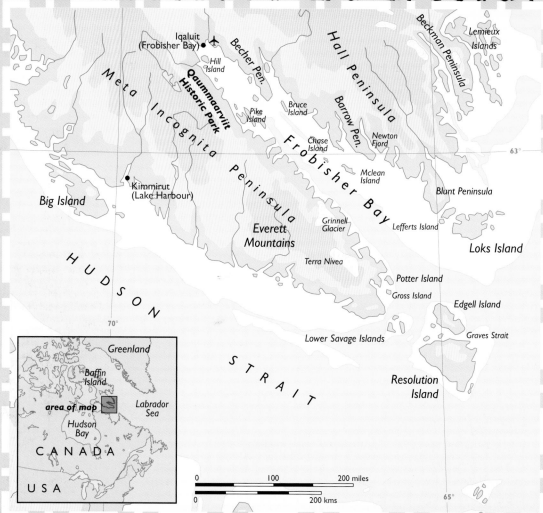

- Iqaluit (Frobisher Bay) ✈
- Becher Pen.
- Hall Peninsula
- Beckman Peninsula
- Lemieux Islands
- Hill Island
- Meta Incognita Peninsula
- Qaummaarviit Historic Park
- Pike Island
- Bruce Island
- Barrow Pen.
- Newton Fjord
- Chase Island
- Mclean Island
- Blunt Peninsula
- Kimmirut (Lake Harbour)
- Big Island
- Frobisher Bay
- Grinnell Glacier
- Lefferts Island
- Loks Island
- Everett Mountains
- Terra Nivea
- Potter Island
- Gross Island
- Edgell Island
- Graves Strait
- HUDSON STRAIT
- 70°
- Lower Savage Islands
- Resolution Island
- 63°
- 65°

- Greenland
- Baffin Island
- area of map
- Labrador Sea
- Hudson Bay
- CANADA
- USA

| 0 | 100 | 200 miles |
| 0 | | 200 kms |

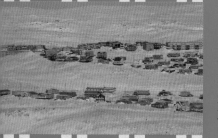

The three-week Serious Arctic expedition took place on Baffin Island in the far north of Canada. The team flew in to Iqaluit, the capital of the territory of Nunavut. Newly created in 1999 as a largely self-governed home for the indigenous Inuit people, Nunavut is one of the least populated areas on Earth. Just 30,000 people live in an area the size of Western Europe.

GLACIER FORMATION

Glaciers are gigantic masses of ice, formed in areas of heavy snowfall. As the snow builds up, the weight pressing down turns layers of snow beneath into ice. Eventually, the mass of ice starts moving slowly down mountains or valleys under its own huge weight. So powerful are glaciers that they have helped to shape our landscape, carving out great valleys in mountain ranges. At lower altitude the ice begins to melt, and over a long period of time the glacier reaches a constant size, as the ice being formed at the top is balanced by the amount lost at the bottom.

This makes glaciers perfect "barometers" for climate change, as a shrinking or expanding glacier is a pretty sure sign the local climate is warming or cooling.

THE SERIOUS ARCTIC GLACIER RESEARCH PROJECT

The Serious Arctic team worked with glaciologists from the Geological Survey of Canada on the first-ever detailed study of the Grinnell Glacier, about 110 km (70 miles) from Iqaluit down Frobisher Bay. The adventurers planted aluminium poles as benchmarks so the scientists could return in the future to check if the glacier is expanding or shrinking. The team also helped take core samples of ice to monitor recent snowfalls and levels of pollution.

Initial results point to the same dramatic shrinking found nearer the North Pole, suggesting global warming is as great even in this southerly part of the Arctic. If confirmed, it's more bad news for the future of the polar bear (see page 24).

WHICH IS WORSE, to be too hot or too cold?

When you're utterly frozen at -40°C (-40°F), a toasty jungle at plus 40°C (104°F) seems hugely appealing. But endure the reality of trekking in 90 percent humidity with your clothes so full of sweat that you could wring them out, and suddenly you find yourself longing for that clean, cool Arctic air.

One Serious Arctic survival expert said he prefers the cold as he can always put on more clothes and jump around to get warm, whereas there's little he can do to cool down if he gets too hot in the jungle. Logically it's hard to argue with that, but many people seem able to acclimate to the heat sooner or later, while they find it hard ever to relax completely in the cold.

Arctic Wildlife

The Arctic is home to a surprisingly wide range of animals, each ingeniously adapted to life in this hostile landscape. Some bugs and beasties can even tolerate being frozen solid, and the short summer brings out a wide variety of insects including mosquitoes.

POLAR BEAR

Found only in the Arctic, the majestic polar bear has become a symbol of the region—and of the effects of climate change. The endangered animal is an excellent swimmer, its relatively small head helping streamline it through the water.

Polar bears eat mainly seals and other marine mammals, and their hunting ground is at the edge of the frozen sea, or on smaller ice floes. While they sometimes stalk their prey on the sea ice, the cunning creatures will often wait patiently for a seal to pop its head up through an air hole in the ice, springing into action to drag it out of the water with its powerful paws.

Humans are their only predator, with hunting for sport and skins reducing numbers dramatically in the last century. Scientists estimate only around twenty-five thousand remain, and while hunting is now strictly controlled, the endangered bears face

a new and critical threat from global warming. With the sea ice shrinking and melting earlier each year, polar bears are finding it ever harder to catch enough food to survive.

ARCTIC FOX

This beautiful creature has the warmest fur of any mammal, and is the only fox to change color with the seasons, making it extremely hard to spot. In winter its fur is almost pure white, turning brown in summer (another variety has a blue-gray coat in winter). Its short ears and legs also help minimize heat loss. The Arctic fox stays active all winter, feeding off small rodents like lemmings and voles. If they're not available it will dig up food buried in more plentiful times, and will also scavenge leftovers from bear kills.

With two layers of fur and a thick layer of blubber, the polar bear is adapted perfectly to the frozen Arctic, losing almost no heat from its body.

The snow white fur of the Arctic fox provides excellent camouflage.

CARIBOU

Caribou are the wild relative of the domesticated reindeer and have adapted to the extreme conditions by making extremely hardy plants, called lichens, the main part of their diet. These plants form a thin covering over rocks, and caribou will dig through the snow with their hooves to find them. They may migrate hundreds of miles, heading to the more southerly parts of the Arctic in winter in search of food.

MUSK OX

The huge musk ox has two coats to keep it warm, an underlayer of fine wool and a much longer, shaggy outer coat. The inner wool coat is far softer and warmer than wool and is often used by local people to weave scarves. Like caribou, musk oxen use their hooves to clear snow so they can graze on lichens and mosses.

BIRDS

Many birds visit the Arctic in summer, from snow geese to the amazing Arctic tern, the greatest traveller in the animal kingdom. This relatively small bird is only around 30 cm (12 in) long, but travels around 40,000 km (25,000 miles) each year, migrating from the Arctic to the Antarctic and back again. In this way it spends summer in each polar region, experiencing almost constant daylight.

SEA MAMMALS

The icy Arctic waters are home to many species of seal, including the polar bear's favorite, the ringed seal. All sea mammals need to surface to breathe, and the ringed seal is able to live under vast areas of frozen ocean by using its sharp claws to cut breathing holes in the ice, which may be several yards thick. This is occasionally its undoing, as it may pop its head up only to find a hungry polar bear lying in wait.

Several types of whale are found only in Arctic waters, including the huge bowhead, named after its bowed lower jaw, and the legendary narwhal. Male narwhals have an extraordinary spiral tusk up to 3 m (10 ft) long, prompting comparisons with the mythical unicorn. The tusk, an extended ivory tooth, is not used for hunting, and its true function remains something of a mystery.

⟨?⟩ HOW DO YOU fight off a polar bear?

With great difficulty, truth be told, so the real answer is never to get into the situation in the first place. Polar bears are the world's largest land carnivores. There are many horrific tales of how they've stalked and attacked humans, unlike, for example, grizzly and black bears, which don't see humans as prey, tending to attack only when surprised or threatened. Despite the horror stories, polar bears also generally avoid people unless they are starving, and fatalities are rare.

An adult male is immensely strong and typically weighs around 350 kg (800 lbs), four times the average adult human. It is essential to have an armed local guide with you who should help you avoid encounters in the first place.

Common sense rules include never approaching a bear for any reason, and avoiding the kill site of a seal or other animal. Choose a campsite well away from bear "highways" and den sites, and pitch your tents wide apart in a line so that a bear wandering into your camp won't feel surrounded and threatened. Husky teams with a track record of scaring away polar bears are always a good deterrent.

If a bear does show signs of stalking and hunting you, there are no guaranteed strategies for scaring it away. It's important to stay together as a group and stand your ground. It may help to make lots of noise by banging pots and pans together and throwing things like firecrackers, but if the animal is very hungry and determined you will have to rely on your armed guide. Sadly, if all else fails, it may ultimately be a case of kill or be killed.

CLIMATE CHANGE AND THE ARCTIC

It is now an accepted fact that the Earth has been warming up in recent years. While there may still be some dispute over how much of the climate change is down to human activity and how much is part of a natural cycle, it is clear that global warming is already having a dramatic effect on the Arctic.

Local studies such as the glacier survey carried out in part by the Serious Arctic team suggest the Arctic is heating up at almost twice the average global rate. The area of frozen sea is shrinking, the spring ice thaw is happening earlier and the autumn freeze later each year. If the temperature continues to rise as scientists predict, there could be devastating consequences for both wildlife and local people.

Taking an ice core sample (above) from the Grinnell Glacier.

An aerial view (left) of spectacular ice formations where the frozen sea meets the open ocean.

Frostbite

Horrendous pictures of blackened fingers and toes mean frostbite is high on the list of concerns when in the Arctic—and with good reason. Many explorers and mountaineers fall victim, especially as frostbite creeps up on you without any real warning or pain (the cold actually numbs the area).

Frostbite is caused when parts of the body get too cold and the skin and flesh literally start to freeze, with ice crystals forming in the tissue. Most at risk are exposed parts such as the face and ears, and extremities like fingers and toes where blood circulation is at its weakest. If caught at the earliest stages frostbite can easily be treated, but otherwise it leads to awful-looking blackened areas, which may need amputating.

FROSTNIP

The first, completely reversible stage of a cold injury is called frostnip, where just the skin is starting to freeze. Signs are waxy-looking pale patches plus slight tingling or numbness. To treat this condition, simply warm up gradually without rubbing. If on your face, take off a glove and rest a warm hand on the area till the color starts to come back. For feet the best solution is to place

HOW CAN YOU stop your face getting frostbite?

It's a scary thought that at -30°C (-22°F) with a wind of 16 km/h (10 mph), your skin can start to freeze in as little as one or two minutes. So if the temperature starts to plummet or an icy wind gets up, the only answer is to make sure no skin whatsoever is exposed.

Of course, in the Arctic nothing is simple, and if you cover all your face you immediately have the problem of your damp breath turning into ice on your face mask, as well as goggles steaming up and freezing over so you can't see.

A neat solution is to customise a pair of goggles by sewing on a nose-guard made of windproof material. It leaves a gap for breathing and protects the nose, one of the most vulnerable areas of all.

CAN SNOW REALLY make you blind?

The glare from snow can cause a very painful condition called snow blindness. You don't actually go blind—it's just too uncomfortable to open your eyes for a day or two.

Snow blindness is effectively sunburn of the eyeball, and, like sunburn, it appears a few hours after exposure to ultraviolet (UV) rays from the Sun. It feels as if you have sand in your eyes, vision becomes blurred, and you become very sensitive to light.

Treatment is to stay in a darkened area with cool bandages over the eyes, taking painkillers and applying special eyedrops until the pain settles down. This can take several days.

To avoid snow blindness, you should always wear either goggles or good wrap-around sunglasses designed to block out UV rays. Don't be fooled by overcast days—the UV light still gets through.

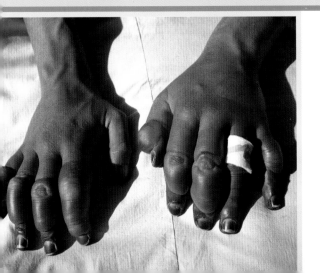

them somewhere warm, like the armpits or groin area of a colleague (this is where buddies truly earn their title!).

Even if the weather's a little "warmer" it's still essential to use the buddy system, where pairs of expedition members watch out for each other. Your partner can immediately warn you if, for example, they see that you have a waxy-looking patch on your face. Pulling lots of faces to exercise the muscles and get blood circulating is also a good idea in cold conditions.

Hypothermia

There comes a point when being "a bit cold" turns into something much more serious. As warm-blooded animals we need to stay at a pretty constant temperature of around 37°C (98°F) for our vital organs to work properly.

The body does an amazing job over a massive range of activities and outside temperatures, but in extreme conditions it may eventually not be able to cope.

It only takes a fall in body temperature of a mere two degrees to around 35°C (95°F) for hypothermia to set in. A victim will feel sluggish and groggy, unable to think or speak clearly, and will suffer from violent shivering as the body tries to generate energy.

If not treated quickly, hypothermia can be fatal. A sure sign it's turning critical is when shivering stops completely. This happens as the body temperature falls further and energy reserves are used up. Everything in the body slows down including the pulse and breathing, so much so that there are cases where people have been assumed to be dead, only to recover completely on rewarming.

TREATMENT FOR HYPOTHERMIA

Firstly, get the victim out of the cold if possible, for example, by putting up a tent to get out of the wind. If they got cold quickly then they probably have only mild hypothermia and can be warmed up pretty fast.

If, however, the casualty's core temperature has fallen below 32°C (90°F) they must be handled extremely gently and discouraged from doing too much to help (there is serious risk of arrhythmia, where the heart stops beating normally). Rewarming should be done very gradually by wrapping the casualty in blankets and giving him warm drinks if possible. The body heat of another person is also effective (ideally by getting into a sleeping bag naked with the victim).

Seek expert medical help as soon as possible and get the casualty to hospital. There, warm fluids may be put into the veins and other areas, such as the chest cavity and abdomen.

WIND CHILL

The "wind chill factor" is often mentioned on weather forecasts nowadays, as it's become recognized that the wind can have a serious effect on how quickly you get cold. Just as you blow on hot food to cool it down, the wind takes away warm air from the surface of your body, cooling you down much more quickly. A chart has been devised by scientists to show what the temperature feels like at various wind speeds. For example, at −9°C (16°F) with a 24 km/h (15 mph) wind, it feels similar to −18°C (−0.4°F) on a still day.

WIND CHILL CHART

TEMPERATURE (°F)

WIND SPEED (MPH)	39	36	30	25	19	16	10	5	0	-6	-9	-15	-20	-26	-29	-35	-40	-45
5	36	30	25	19	12	7	1	-6	-11	-17	-22	-27	-35	-40	-45	-53	-56	-63
10	34	27	21	16	9	3	-4	-9	-17	-22	-27	-35	-42	-47	-53	-60	-65	-72
15	15	25	19	12	7	0	-8	-13	-18	-26	-33	-38	-45	-51	-58	-63	-71	-78
20	30	25	18	10	5	-2	-9	-15	-22	-34	-35	-42	-47	-54	-61	-67	-74	-81
25	30	23	16	9	3	-4	-11	-17	-11	-35	-36	-44	-51	-58	-63	-71	-78	-83
30	28	21	16	9	1	-6	-11	-18	-15	-36	-38	-45	-53	-60	-67	-72	-80	-87
35	28	21	14	7	0	-8	-15	-20	-17	-37	-42	-47	-54	-61	-67	-76	-81	-89
40	27	19	12	7	0	-8	-15	-22	-20	-38	-44	-51	-56	-63	-71	-78	-83	-90
45	27	19	12	5	-2	-9	-17	-24	-29	-38	-44	-51	-58	-65	-72	-80	-87	-92
50	27	19	12	3	-2	-9	-17	-24	-31	-39	-45	-53	-60	-67	-74	-81	-89	-96
55	25	18	10	5	-2	-11	-18	-26	-33	-39	-45	-54	-61	-67	-74	-81	-89	-98
60	25	18	10	3	-4	-11	-18	-26	-33	-40	-47	-54	-61	-67	-76	-83	-90	-98

The numbers in the colored areas of the chart represent how cold it feels at various temperatures and wind speeds.

Danger of frostbite
- Low risk
- Exposed skin starts to freeze in around 5–10 mins
- Exposed skin starts to freeze in around 1–2 mins
- Exposed skin starts to freeze in around 30 secs

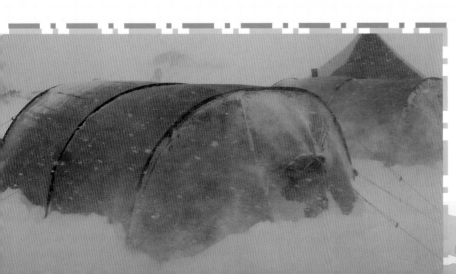

A strong wind can make temperatures seem much colder than they really are.

The author filming Serious Arctic in temperatures of around –30˚C (–22˚F).

 # DOES MINUS FIFTY really feel any colder than minus ten or twenty?

A good question—once you're absolutely freezing, how can you possibly feel any colder? It's really about the ability to keep warm and how quickly you are in trouble. You can almost feel the heat being sucked out of your body at extreme low temperatures. All the clothes in the world don't seem to keep you warm without a lot of leaping about, and frostbite and hypothermia can quickly set in.

WHY IS IT dangerous to sweat?

Surprisingly, one of the key problems in the freezing Arctic is getting hot and sweaty (all too easy when you're wrapped from head to toe in layer upon layer of clothing). Odd though it first seems, getting too hot means you quickly get too cold.

The reason is that if you let yourself sweat, the perspiration freezes within seconds. You then have a layer of ice next to your skin, which means you are on a slippery slope to frostbite and hypothermia. In short: you sweat—you die!

That's why layering is so important (see page 34), removing or putting on layers of clothes as necessary. All experienced Arctic adventurers start the day with the minimum number of layers on. Although they may feel cold for a few minutes, they know the strenuous activity ahead will soon warm them.

SMALL MISTAKE, BIG PROBLEM

Take extra care not to spill water or other liquid on your gloves or other vital bits of clothing. The resulting frozen item of clothing will be all but useless and will take a lot of time and effort to sort out, either heating and drying it above a stove or taking it with you inside your sleeping bag overnight (see page 52).

If you ignore the problem, you may again be on the route to serious cold injuries. Letting snow get inside your gloves will have similar effects. The heat of your hands will melt it, the water will turn into ice and off you'll go again down that slippery slope.

Pulling pulks across the sea ice is a constant juggle between overheating and possible hypothermia and frostbite.

Arctic Clothing

Getting your clothing right is critical in the Arctic. You need to be thinking constantly about what you're wearing, adding or taking off layers to make sure you never get too cold—or too hot (see page 30).

Clothes largely keep you warm by trapping air to insulate you, and the principle is to wear lots of thinner layers rather than a couple of really thick ones. This way you can adjust your temperature more easily.

As you first put on your underwear and thermals, it's a sobering thought that you may well not change them for the entire expedition. Somehow, the complex logistics of changing pants at −30°C (−22°F) doesn't often seem worth it.

Everyone has their favorite expedition clothing that they feel most comfortable with, and as long as you keep to the basic principles it really doesn't matter.

The kit used in Serious Arctic is "modeled" below by two of the young adventurers. On their feet they wore two pairs of socks and special "moon" boots. Legs had three layers: thermal leggings, trekking pants, and windproof over-trousers.

Their top half was covered in up to six layers: two thermal vests, a thin fleece, Arctic hoodie, windproof jacket with fur round the hood, and a thick puffer jacket.

Finally the neck and head was protected by a neck warmer, balaclava, "head-over" scarf, hat, goggles, and hood. It's important to cover your head at all times to prevent heat loss—once you're dressed, more than one-third of the body's heat is lost via your head. Goggles can be customized with a nose-guard. If "warm" enough not to wear goggles, a good pair of sunglasses which block UV-rays is a must to avoid snow blindness.

Protect your hands with one or two pairs of gloves plus some outer mitts. Thin inner gloves are a good idea for smaller jobs like taking photos. Bare hands will be aching with the cold and going numb in seconds, and will stick to metal as the moisture on your skin freezes on contact with the cold surface.

When fully bundled up, some people feel quite claustrophobic. Everyday tasks like going to the bathroom become a major logistical exercise (see page 54).

When everyone's in full Arctic gear, it's a real problem to figure out who's who.

IS IT POSSIBLE to stay warm in temperatures as low as minus fifty?

It may seem unlikely, especially when you can go outside back home and feel freezing in temperatures well above zero, but it is certainly achievable. The truth is that most people don't wear the right clothes to keep them warm in their everyday lives (usually being more concerned about fashion).

In the Arctic it's rather more crucial to be really clued up. The key is to use lots of layers, trapping air between your clothes for insulation, and to cover up all exposed flesh when the weather gets seriously cold. In extreme low temperatures it's important not to let yourself even start to get chilled as it's much harder to get warm again.

HOW DO YOU stop your feet getting cold?

A real worry, as anyone who's stood around waiting for a bus on an icy winter's day will know. Whatever footwear you've got on, the heat eventually seems to just drain away into the pavement.

But the good news is that special "moon" boots have been developed for use in extreme conditions. With thick rubber insulating soles and separate felt liners, they'll keep your feet warm down to a reassuringly low -100°C (-148°F), colder even than the Arctic.

COLD COMFORT

The object of the layering system is to keep the heat in and the icy wind out, and to allow your body to "breathe," preventing the build-up of perspiration (damp clothes next to your skin have almost no insulating properties). Fit is crucial. Too tight and the clothes won't allow a layer of air next to the skin; too loose and there will be too much air to warm up effectively.

Inner layer(s)   Thermals with good wicking properties. This means they actually take moisture away from the skin and transfer it to their outer surface without the thermals themselves getting wet. Avoid cotton, which gets too damp.

Middle layer(s)   Fleece to keep you warm (modern fleeces will again continue "wicking" moisture away from your body).

Outer layer   Windproofs to keep out the biting polar wind.

Extra layer   Extremely warm clothing, for example, thick puffer jacket, usually only for use when stopped outside to prevent getting chilled.

The Frozen Ocean

The Arctic Ocean is one of the wonders of the world, made up of vast, ever-changing masses of ice floating on the sea beneath. As ice sheets shift in the wind and current they collide to form pressure ridges, spectacular areas of ice which may be several yards high—and often extremely difficult for adventurers to cross.

As the ice drifts or breaks up it leaves dangerous cracks or open areas of sea. The ice can vary greatly in thickness, ranging from about 0.5–4 m (roughly 2–14 ft).

Around half the Arctic Ocean stays frozen all year, with parts nearer the edge of the Arctic Circle melting in spring and refreezing in the autumn.

PACK ICE OR ICE FLOE?

Huge, fairly continuous sheets of sea ice are known as pack ice, while smaller free-floating chunks less than around 8 km (5 miles) wide are called ice floes. Huge icebergs that have broken away from glaciers can also be found floating in the Arctic Ocean.

The Serious Arctic training camp on the sea ice in the middle of Frobisher Bay in April.

HOW DO YOU travel about on the frozen ocean?

You might wonder why anyone ventures onto the frozen ocean in the first place. There are in fact a variety of reasons:

- In mountainous regions with difficult terrain the frozen ocean is like a "highway," providing faster, direct routes to other areas
- For adventurers it's often the only way to reach their goal, including the North Pole itself
- Local people need to head onto the sea ice to fish and hunt for animals like seals and polar bears

The traditional way of traveling across the frozen ocean is by dogsled (see page 40), replaced in recent times in many areas by the snowmobile.

If traveling under your own steam the best way to take your kit is by pulling a small sledge called a pulk behind you. It's the stuff of real polar exploration and is actually not as hard as it looks—until you hit the nightmare of pressure ridges. Stopping when going downhill back on the frozen land is also quite an art.

WHY DOESN'T the frozen sea crack up when the tide comes in?

To an extent it does. Each day the sea ice may rise or fall by several metres with the tides. At the shoreline the frozen sea is stuck fast to the land (it's actually known as fast ice for that reason), so something's got to give. Usually it means long cracks appear in the ice, perhaps about 100 m (300 ft) from the shore, where the ice "hinges" up or down and eventually breaks. The open water will usually refreeze quickly, but it can be a treacherous area to travel over.

–?–HOW CAN YOU check if the ice is strong enough to walk on?

The short answer is that unless you're an expert you can't. Sea ice and frozen lakes are incredibly dangerous, and while there are safety pointers like the color of the ice (clear blue or green ice is usually stronger), this is definitely one to leave to an experienced local guide. They will know the hazards. For example, snow may be hiding a weak area of sea ice regularly cracked by the tides.

As a general rule, a layer of ice less than 10 cm (4 in) thick is too thin to walk on, but even ice much thicker may have unseen weak spots and could quickly change depending on the conditions. Getting across successfully is absolutely no guarantee the ice will still be safe an hour or two later.

WHAT HAPPENS IF the ice cracks and you fall in?

This is guaranteed to be one of the less pleasant experiences in life—and could all too easily end it. The water under the ice is around freezing point (if it's the sea rather than a freshwater lake, it may actually be a degree or two below zero as saltwater has a lower freezing point).

Your body's reflex reaction to hitting the ice cold water is involuntary gasping. If at all possible, keep your head above water and/or cover your mouth to avoid taking in water and drowning. You will feel winded and hyperventilate, fighting to catch your breath. The natural instinct is to panic, desperately trying to get out as quickly as possible. This is understandable but usually serves only to increase the chances of drowning.

Just concentrate on staying afloat and getting your breath back. It may take a couple of minutes, but you should have a good five minutes before you become too cold and weak to help yourself. Then look around for a firm enough bit of ice to get your arms and chest out of the water—often where you fell in is best. It can be very difficult to heave yourself out onto the slippery ice, so once you've got your arms out get into a horizontal swimming position, kicking your legs to help crawl forward onto the ice.

Don't try to stand up as the ice may be very weak. Keep lying down so your weight is spread out, and roll well away from the edge.

Even if you can't get out, don't panic. You can survive for at least fifteen minutes, possibly over an hour, and hopefully there will be someone nearby to help rescue you.

Your rescuers will, of course, have to be very careful not to fall in themselves. If possible they should stay well away from the edge, passing you a long branch or a rope with a big loop to put under your arms (you will be pretty numb by now).

If all has gone well you will have only mild hypothermia, but will still need to be warmed up (see page 30).

Sled Dogs

As they whisk you through some of the planet's most inhospitable landscape, these magnificent dogs really do feel like a human's best friend. Sled dogs have been bred over thousands of years for stamina and hard work in Arctic conditions. They have two layers of fur for insulation and are at their happiest running for hours on end in the freezing cold pulling a heavy load. Most breeds can manage up to twice their own weight.

BREEDS OF SLED DOG

Although sometimes referred to just as huskies, there are in fact several different types of sled dog. They are among the oldest breeds of dog in the world.

The beautiful Samoyed originates from Siberia in the Russian Arctic and is well insulated from the cold by its extremely thick fur.

The Siberian husky comes from a different part of Siberia and has a much sleeker outer coat. It can have penetrating blue eyes.

The Alaskan Malamute is a particularly large and hardy sled dog, bred originally in Alaska.

Pure Canadian Inuit dogs are in danger of dying out, with sadly just a few hundred individuals left. This was the main breed used by the Serious Arctic team.

CONTROLLING SLED DOGS

A sled dog driver is known as a musher, and it's important to adopt a very firm tone when giving the dogs commands. Sled dogs have not been bred as pets and can be quite a handful, but they will look up to a strong, dominant musher as the head of the pack.

SLED DOG COMMANDS

Hike	Start moving or go faster
Jee	Go to the right
Haw	Go to the left
On by	Go straight on ignoring turns or distractions
Easy	Go slower
Whoa	Stop
Mush	Rarely used by mushers except in movies!

A team of Canadian Inuit dogs prepare to spend the night chained out on the sea ice (right).

WHY DON'T sled dogs' feet get frostbite?

Sled dogs are very well insulated with thickly padded paws and fur in between the toes. There are other adaptations as well, which are thought to keep lots of blood flowing through the feet and help keep the tissue from freezing.

The booties often seen on huskies' feet are not primarily to keep them warm, but to keep the dogs from getting cuts when they are traveling over rough ice.

There are several ways dogs can be hitched up to the sled. Among the most common are the fan hitch, fanning out in front of the sled, or the tandem hitch, paired up in a line, which is better for narrow trails.

The dogs work together as a pack, and it's essential to choose the right lead dog(s) to set the pace for the others and help find the best route through the snow.

Sled dogs need to be chained out in a line overnight so they don't run off. The trick when out on expedition is securing the line by putting large ice screws firmly into the ice.

The sled dogs will be happy to sleep outside in the Arctic chill, even if there is a blizzard raging. They will often burrow down into the snow for insulation. If available, raw seal meat is one of their favorite foods.

There is little more exhilarating than running a team of sled dogs in the most spectacular terrain. Unfortunately, as snowmobiles take over for most Arctic transport, working sled dogs are becoming rarer. Most of the faster breeds are now used mainly for sled dog racing.

A sled dog never forgets

Crossing a frozen lake during the Serious Arctic expedition, the sled dogs began to get very jittery and eventually refused to continue. Some even leapt onto the sled. According to their local musher, the dogs were agitated because a previous attempt to cross the same lake had led to a soaking when the ice gave way.

Food and Water

Carting bulky food and gallons of water on expedition is always a non-starter, and in the Arctic it's particularly pointless as everything would quickly be frozen solid. So apart from a few treats, freeze-dried expedition rations, pasta and porridge are probably the answer. You just need to add water. This raises the obvious question—where does the water come from? The answer of course is the endless supply of snow.

MELTING SNOW

This is one of the most essential—and tedious—jobs on an Arctic expedition, easily taking two or three hours every day.

First you need to fill a trash bag with chunks of fairly solid, compressed snow (don't take powdery stuff from the surface). The old cliché "don't eat yellow snow" applies, so camp discipline in having well-defined pee and poo spots really pays off.

Then it's simply a case of stuffing endless small amounts of the snow into a saucepan, prodding and stirring constantly. Put a little water in first, otherwise much of the snow will be lost as steam and the pan will burn.

Snow is full of air, and depending on how densely the original snow is packed together, you will get at best about one-third as much water (it might even be as little as one-tenth). The water produced will be all you have for drinking and cooking. After so much effort you probably won't want to "waste" any for cleaning and washing—small chunks of snow will do fine for this.

THE ARCTIC DESERT

It's one of those strange facts about the Arctic that it's actually a desert. In the Arctic, rainfall and snowfall combined comes to less than 25 cm (10 in) of water. This qualifies it as a desert region, though scientists make the distinction between hot and cold deserts.

It also feels incredibly dry; cold air has hardly any moisture in it. This means that as you breathe, you feel very parched.

In these conditions dehydration is a serious problem. It's hard to force yourself to keep drinking when it's so cold and can be such an effort to get liquid, but you'll need at least 5 litres (1 gallon) a day to cope with all the exertion of an expedition.

HOW DO YOU take something with you to drink? Won't it just freeze?

This is a rather crucial question that may not even cross your mind unless you've been to the Arctic. The fact is that in temperatures way below zero, just about all liquids freeze (even mercury used in thermometers freezes at around -39°C/-38°F).

So this is where a rugged vacuum flask comes into its own. It will keep water cold all day without freezing, though on an Arctic expedition it's best to put a hot drink in it to help keep you warm.

DRINK YOUR HOT WATER BOTTLE!

One trick for avoiding dehydration is to drink the water in your hot water bottle. When you go to bed it's great to have a sturdy plastic bottle filled with hot water to keep your feet warm. By morning it'll be pretty cold, and instead of wasting the precious water, force yourself to drink it all. You'll already be getting dehydrated after a night breathing dry, cold air, and it'll get the day off on the right foot (no pun intended).

THE ARCTIC DIET

Most polar explorers come back far lighter than they started, a result of the huge effort involved in most activities, plus the energy used in keeping warm. A male adventurer may use up more than five thousand calories a day in the Arctic—double what he needs on a typical day back in "civilization." To stay the same weight he would have to eat the equivalent of about eighty slices of bread each day.

So you need to eat a lot, and in particular a lot of carbohydrates for energy—a great excuse to eat plenty of chocolate and sugar (though a frozen bar of chocolate will need to be warmed in an inside pocket before you can bite into it). While most expedition food will inevitably be stuff you add water to, take along a little "real" food to thaw out for special occasions. It's amazing what a bit of bacon, sausage, or salami can do for morale.

Working in the Arctic

It's one thing to survive in such a hostile environment, but it's quite another to contemplate actually working. Swathed in endless layers of clothes, worrying about getting too hot or cold, and with all your liquids freezing solid, working effectively is a massive challenge. As with most things in the Arctic, you have to be incredibly organized and allow lots of time to do the smallest thing.

HOT TIPS FOR COLD CONDITIONS

- Take lots of disposable chemical hand-warmers, which begin to heat as soon as they're taken out of their airtight packet and last for five or six hours. Placed between inner layers of gloves, they will keep your hands nice and warm, along with anything else you store there. On particularly cold days they can also be placed between layers of socks.

- Searching pockets for your camera/sunglasses/compass while wearing three layers of gloves at −40°C (−40°F) is not good news. Work out a system for where everything goes in your clothes and backpack pockets—and stick to it.

- Losing an essential piece of kit like a glove will ruin your trip and may lead to serious cold injuries. Avoid misplacing bulky outer mitts by tying them together with a long cord. Then thread the cord through the arms of your jacket like a schoolchild. If you want to do something in a hurry, you can whip the bulky mitts off without worrying.

- Take only a small digital camera. If there's a dial with lots of different arty settings, tape over the buttons—otherwise it'll probably get turned accidentally as you wrestle your camera out of a pocket, ruining a once-in-a-lifetime photo opportunity. Small dials and buttons are almost impossible to use with gloves on anyway.

The Serious expedition was stormbound for three days on the sea ice in an Arctic blizzard.

- Disposable alkaline batteries are hopeless at low temperatures. Use lithium or if possible rechargeable batteries for all electronic gadgets like cameras and GPS handsets. Even these will go dead alarmingly fast in the cold, so keep the devices warm in an inside pocket, perhaps adding a hand-warmer, until the moment you need them. Keep a couple of spare batteries tucked in your gloves.

FILMING SERIOUS ARCTIC

Making a major "fly-on-the-wall" documentary series, the filming team didn't have the luxury of sitting around waiting for cold cameras to get to tent temperature and stop steaming up. And they certainly couldn't afford to have them ice up if they needed to quickly run out of a tent. The only answer was to have two sets of cameras—one for outside and one for in.

? HOW DO YOU avoid your glasses steaming up when you go into a tent?

A big question with sadly no easy answer. While tents are likely to be far from room temperature they will almost always be warmer than anything coming in from outside, so any moisture in the air inside the tent will immediately condense on glasses, camera lenses and so on (just as the cold windshield of a car will steam up on a winter's morning).

If you want to take pictures inside, you just have to wait till the camera has warmed up to the temperature of the tent.

Whatever you do, don't let your glasses steam up and then immediately head back outside. The moisture will freeze in seconds, leaving you to scrape the ice off the specs before you can see, or in the case of a camera possibly putting it out of action for the rest of the trip.

As a tent was erected, a film camera would be deposited inside so it was always at the ambient temperature. Camera operators filming in the open could then follow a story inside by leaving their cold camera outside by the door, and picking up the "inside" camera as they entered the tent—with no danger of it steaming up. Similarly, they could run back outside if needed and pick up the "outside" camera to carry on filming.

There is certainly no polar filming guidebook with perfect solutions to every problem. Each Arctic camera operator has favored compromises, for example, a battery pack strapped inside their body with a lead to the film camera. This helps keep the batteries warm so they last longer, but may be very awkward for filming. Similarly, some use heated camera jackets, which feel great as you poke your hands through special sleeves to get at the controls. However, they may be hugely frustrating as you flounder around trying to film a one-off incident in a hurry.

⊕?─CAN YOU stop all your lotions and potions from freezing?

Only if they're somewhere warm, which basically means tucking anything that might freeze inside your clothes near to your body, or thawing them out overnight by taking them into your sleeping bag with you. Backpacks or cases will be well below zero whether inside your tent or not, and anything left in them will be frozen solid.

This means some careful thought about what to take on the expedition. For example, do you need shampoo, deodorant, and all those creams? (Most would say not—you won't be doing much by way of washing.) And what about toothpaste? (Many would say yes, feeling that fresh breath is worth the space taken up by the tube in the sleeping bag.)

WILL CONTACT LENSES freeze to your eyes?

A common worry, but actually highly unlikely. As soon as the temperature plummets, you should hopefully be wearing goggles, which will keep the icy wind off your eyes. More likely is for eyes to freeze shut as a result of them watering in the cold and the eyelashes freezing together. A warm hand placed over the eye will soon thaw it out.

Contact lenses are actually more practical in the Arctic than glasses, which are awkward to wear under goggles and are forever steaming up and freezing over. Not to say that lenses don't have their own problems. Keeping fluids and unused lenses from freezing is another logistical nightmare.

The temperature inside the Serious Arctic base camp, erected on the frozen sea, rarely crept above freezing point. First job in the morning was scraping the ice off the ceiling.

Tents and Igloos

After a hard day on the ice at -40°C (-40°F) with an Arctic gale blowing, there's nothing quite like the thought of getting back inside your tent. The only slight problem is that if you're on the move you'll first have to put it up. And don't imagine your sleeping tent is going to be warm and toasty like a room back home. If you're lucky it might be no colder than a freezer.

Choose a tent designed to withstand Arctic storms, and before the expedition begins practice putting it up quickly with thick mitts on. You might have to do it for real in atrocious weather.

The polar pyramid tents below, used in Serious Arctic, are large enough to allow some cooking.

Flaps at ground level round the tent are piled up with snow to help anchor it in the wind.

Guy ropes are secured with ice screws on the frozen sea (which is covered here in a layer of snow). On deep snow away from the sea they may be attached to a buried ski pole or other improvised anchor (known as a "deadman"). A top tip is to pee in the snow above the "deadman"— as the pee freezes it helps make it more secure.

STOVES

Using stoves in small tents can be very dangerous (one for the experts only), so all melting of snow and cooking will probably be done in a larger, main expedition tent. The goods news is that as a result this tent may get pretty warm in the evening. But fuel is precious and likely to be in short supply. This means once supper is over the stoves will go off for the night and the temperature will plummet.

Note that whenever stoves are on there is serious risk of fire—and carbon monoxide poisoning. Although it may go against the grain when it's so cold outside, it's absolutely vital to ensure there is enough ventilation.

Losing daylight isn't a problem when putting up tents in the Arctic: in early spring the sun is already setting well into the evening.

WHICH IS WARMER—a tent or an igloo?

It may seem unlikely, but there's no doubt that igloos are far warmer and cozier to sleep in—and also much quieter than tents which flap and howl in the wind. While a tent will be almost as cold as the air outside (perhaps −30°C (−22°F) or lower), the temperature overnight in an igloo can be a cosy 0°C (32°F) or even just above.

So how is this possible? The key is that snow is a great insulator, being full of tiny air pockets. Bodies, candles, and cooking will heat up the igloo, and it will then stay well above the outside temperature all night.

Which raises the obvious question—won't candles and cooking make the igloo melt and collapse? Again, surprisingly, the answer is no. As the igloo heats up, a thin inside layer of snow will melt, only for some of it to be turned to ice by the cold layer of snow beyond. This will actually make the structure stronger.

As part of expedition training, the Serious Arctic team had the choice of whether to sleep in a tent or an igloo. Those who chose the igloo had a much more comfortable night.

ARCTIC SARDINES

Many campers traditionally subtract one from the number of people a tent is claimed to sleep. So if, for example, it's described as a three-person tent, they know it'll comfortably sleep two plus all their kit. In the Arctic, however, packing the maximum number of people into the tent will definitely feel warmer at night. On the down side, it can be especially difficult to stay organized with so little personal space.

BUILDING AN IGLOO

Igloos are remarkably efficient and have been perfected over centuries by the Inuit peoples:

- They are best constructed from blocks of solid, compressed snow. These are far easier to work with than blocks of solid ice and make a much warmer igloo.
- If the snow is not solid enough to form strong blocks, get the team to stamp on an area for half an hour to compress it. Then leave it for a short while to refreeze.
- Blocks are cut from the snow using a snow saw or knife.
- It's a good design feature to build the igloo round a hole left by the blocks, as it will give you shelves to sit and sleep on. The sleeping platforms will then benefit from the warmest air in the igloo. (Warm air rises while the heavier, colder air sinks to the bottom.)
- The blocks are built up in a spiral, facing slightly inwards; each layer of blocks is overlapped for strength as when building a brick wall. The blocks get smaller and more triangular the higher you go.
- Make your entrance before putting on the top blocks!
- The final block can be lowered in and shaped from inside to make a snug fit. This last block makes the igloo structure strong.
- Fill in gaps by shovelling on snow and gently packing it into the cracks.
- Cut one or two ventilation holes in the igloo, and don't completely cover the doorway.

For more Inuit survival techniques, see page 60.

The team members attempt to build their first igloo.

Having built an igloo in bitterly cold conditions, team spirits were lifted by traditional Inuit throat singing.

The igloo provides the team with some welcome warmth as the sun goes down.

Sleeping in the Freezer

There are few more miserable experiences than spending an entire night utterly exhausted but unable to sleep because you're freezing cold. It can happen all too easily in the Arctic, but with careful preparation and planning you can have a great night's sleep, even when you're effectively sleeping in a freezer—or worse.

CHOOSING A SLEEPING BAG

It goes without saying that you need to splash out on a top-rated sleeping bag good to around −40°C/−40°F (there's no wind chill to add in inside a tent). Even then, many will slot this into an outer "bivi" bag for extra insulation.

Many modern sleeping bags designed for Arctic conditions come in what is known as the "mummy" style, so named because they make you look like an Egyptian mummy. Your body fits in snugly, with a hood area that can be tightened round your face using a drawstring.

The Arctic nightmare of wet stuff freezing rears its head once more. Breathing and sweating in the night produce moisture. If this gets into the material of your sleeping bag, it will of course freeze during the day, leaving you in deep trouble. So you should also use a vapor barrier attached to the inside of the sleeping bag.

Arctic sleeping bags come in different sizes. As with your clothing you want a snug fit because too much air around you will not stay warm. Also hugely important is what you sleep on—it must insulate you from the cold beneath. Use a couple of layers; for example, a ridged roll mat plus a thin, blow-up mat.

HOW DO YOU stay warm in bed at minus thirty?

Obviously, having the right sleeping bag and roll mat(s) are crucial but they won't do the trick on their own. You need to add some serious preparation and organization. Your bedtime routine can easily last half an hour or more. Here is a typical countdown to sleep:

20 Use a sturdy plastic drinking bottle as a hot water bottle. Make sure it has an ultra-reliable top as spills in your sleeping bag are a disaster. Place it in your sleeping bag about 20 minutes before you get in.

19 Make sure you are feeling warm yourself. If you go to bed at all chilled you will never get warm again, so if necessary go for a late night jog around camp.

18 You don't want to get snow on your sleeping bag— or tent groundsheet if you have one—so go into the tent backwards, plonking your bottom on the sleeping bag. Snowy boots should still be poking out of the end of the main tent. Take off the boots and bash snow off. Leave them under cover and remove felt liners to go in your sleeping bag.

17 Take off a few layers—you don't want to actually overheat and sweat—but leave on some socks and perhaps a thin layer of gloves.

16 Place your heavy outer jacket over the bottom end of the sleeping bag for extra insulation.

15 Maneuver your feet round into the sleeping bag before they start to chill.

14 Now is the time to think about all the things you're going to take to bed with you. This includes any liquids and any damp clothing that you don't want to be frozen solid by morning—a damp glove left out will be stiff as a board and absolutely useless.

13 Shove in a small bag with toiletries and personal items such as toothpaste, contact lenses and solutions, creams, and medications.

12 Put in a larger soft bag with damp clothes like gloves, neck warmer, and hats.

11 Don't forget a bottle of drinking water for when you wake up parched in the middle of the night.

10 Men and boys can also add a pee bottle for their convenience (not without hazards—see page 55).

9 Put your boot liners around the hot water bottle to avoid it burning your feet.

8 A bit of a luxury, but crack open a few chemical hand-warmers. Place one in the small of your back, and perhaps reserve another for any other area that feels cold.

7 Make sure your flashlight can easily be located inside your sleeping bag.

6 Your face will need to be partially exposed to the air to allow you to breathe, but should be covered as much as possible. Everyone has their own preference, but you could place a "head-over" scarf on your head and pull it down over your eyes and nose; then pull up a neck warmer over your mouth, leaving only your nostrils exposed. Some find this too restricting, relying instead on a "mummy" sleeping bag with a drawstring that can be pulled tight around the head area.

5 You are finally ready to ease yourself down into the sleeping bag—if there's still room.

4 Zip up and tighten drawstring (if fitted).

3 Spend several minutes struggling to rearrange everything comfortably around you in the sleeping bag—bags designed for Arctic conditions are deliberately made pretty tight.

2 Drive out intense feelings of claustrophobia.

1 Feel snug and a little smug as the polar wind howls outside.

Arctic Toilets

HOW DO YOU pee/poo in the Arctic?

The answer of course is very quickly! You'll be out in the open in what might well be a freezing gale, but as long as you don't linger too long there is thankfully very little danger of frostbite.

Once again it's all about preparation. Think about how to do things efficiently in a hurry—taking gloves off, where you'll put them, where you're going to keep toilet paper and antiseptic handwipes or gel (another item which will quickly freeze). Then simply scrape away a top layer of snow with a shovel and away you go, covering it back over afterwards.

Privacy is a problem on the flat sea ice. It's important for the expedition leaders or local guide to choose a safe area with no thin ice, close to camp so you can always find your way back. If you're lucky you'll be near a pressure ridge with ice rubble to hide behind. It's also essential to keep to set areas, so you don't have the dreaded problem of yellow snow when it comes to melting snow for water. Among all your other concerns, keep an eye out for polar bears.

It's one of the few opportunities to wash your nether regions, so a good idea is to abandon toilet paper and use a snow wedge instead. This is nowhere near as bad as it sounds, and if you haven't taken too long about it all you'll have a lovely clean, tingling sensation around the area when you cover up.

You also avoid the hassle of disposing of toilet paper. Many expedition teams decide not to bury paper but to carry it all out of the area for environmental reasons, which means being very organized with zip-up plastic bags.

WILL MY pee freeze as I go to the bathroom?

Like all liquids in the Arctic it certainly will be frozen before long. But the cartoon image of an arch of pee freezing all the way back to your body is not going to happen—the hot liquid will take a little longer to freeze solid.

There is, however, another related problem worth bearing in mind. If you're trekking long distances directly into the polar wind the groin area is an undoubted candidate for frostbite, especially for men. Metal zippers may get ice cold or let wind through, and you can end up with frostbite in the last place you'd ever want it.

This is exactly what happened to one competitor in a race to the magnetic North Pole, and amid a few raised eyebrows he had to be urgently air-lifted out. To prevent this most unfortunate of cold injuries, sew a patch of windproof material over the appropriate area of your underpants. It's well worth the time and effort!

THE HAZARDS OF PEE BOTTLES

It's the middle of the night. It's minus thirty. You wake desperate for a pee. For females there's now the awful prospect of struggling out of your sleeping bag, but the men and boys have got it easy. You just reach for your pee bottle. What could be simpler?

Well, if you've already used it earlier in the night the first issue is opening it without spilling any of the contents. You then need to maneuver to make sure—how to put this delicately—that things are where they need to be before starting to pee. As the bottle fills you have to listen carefully to the sound changing pitch to make sure it isn't going to overflow. And of course you must screw the cap back on tightly. If all has gone well you've got another hot water bottle!

Finally, don't forget to empty it out immediately in the morning, otherwise you'll have a bottle of frozen urine to deal with (looking for all the world like a new popsicle flavor).

Unfortunately, things didn't go quite so smoothly for one of the Serious Arctic adventurers. He was so exhausted that after he finished his pee he immediately fell asleep—without putting the top back securely on the bottle. It took several hours to wash and dry the offending sleeping bag and clothes.

And then there's the following scenario. It's the middle of the night. It's minus thirty. You wake desperate for a drink. You reach for your water bottle.

Unfortunately in the dark, you've confused it with your pee bottle . . .

CAN YOU "go" in your tent?

It is certainly possible, even if it's not very sociable. Assuming you can get the tent to yourself, you can poo straight into a plastic bag. Once you're back outside your poo will soon freeze and can easily be emptied in the toilet area, or put in the main poo bag if you're carrying waste out with you.

Also, despite not having the "luxury" of the pee bottle, females who need a pee in the middle of the night can avoid leaving the tent completely. If the tent has a porch area for storage, this will probably have no groundsheet. You can pee straight into the snow, confident in the knowledge that it will quickly freeze and won't smell at all. If you wish, you can cover the yellow stains with a fresh layer of snow for cosmetic reasons.

There is also a special device designed to allow females to pee standing up. Called a "Shewee" it takes a bit of practice in the bath or shower, but if and when you feel confident it can be used to pee into a bottle.

WHEN YOU GOTTA GO, YOU GOTTA GO

In such extreme conditions it's very tempting to put off going to the toilet. Don't. One Serious Arctic team member said he'd decided before the expedition to try to go for a poo just once a week. This is not good for you. Force yourself to go when you need to, and you'll feel great after. It'll be a weight off your mind.

LEAVING YOUR MARK

An important decision for the expedition is whether you also need to carry out the poo itself. When the Serious Arctic team went to help survey the Grinnell Glacier, less than a dozen people had ever walked on it before, and the expedition was required to bring out all solid waste to avoid polluting such a pristine environment.

This meant setting up a communal "double-bagged" toilet with two strong trash bags. It also meant peeing in a separate area, which some found tricky ("frozen pee" in the poo bag would weigh too much).

The good news is that the toilet bag isn't as smelly as you might imagine in the sub-zero temperatures, but removing it is still one of the least popular jobs in camp.

Extreme Arctic Weather

The Arctic isn't just indescribably cold. It also has some of the most extreme weather on Earth. Antarctica is actually even worse, though that's pretty academic when you're battling hundred mile an hour Arctic winds at -30°C (-22°F).

Alongside all the usual expedition emergency planning (see page 10), you will need to prepare to be stuck for days in an Arctic blizzard with no way of being evacuated. Before the main Serious Arctic expedition, the leadership team hired a ski plane to put in food and fuel dumps, or "caches," along the expedition route. Polar bear-proof metal containers were used, enabling re-supplies during the expedition. This ensured that when the inevitable blizzards struck there were enough reserve supplies to sit it out.

HOW DO YOU stop your tents from blowing away in a storm?

Storms can hit without any warning, so every time you put your tent up—no matter how cold or exhausted you are - you must ensure it's done properly, with guy ropes anchored firmly and enough snow shoveled over snow flaps. The tiniest rip in a tent must be fixed immediately, otherwise it could be torn to pieces in a storm.

Even so it can be very scary to be woken by the almighty noise of an Arctic gale hitting the camp. The usual first reaction is that there is no way the tent will hold. In fact it almost always will, but in the rare event the tent starts to be ripped apart, you'll have to prepare to abandon it.

Dress in full Arctic gear and if possible drop the tent to the ground so it won't be blown away. Hopefully, there will be other tents managing to weather the storm that your guide will lead you to (do not start wandering around on your own). The rest of the night may be a bit of a tight squeeze, but it's preferable to having to build an emergency snow shelter in a raging storm.

If you do get warning that a storm is on the way, for example, through a satellite phone call to the nearest weather service, build up a snow wall to help protect your tent.

HOW DO YOU find your way in a blizzard?

Don't even try. You could be just a few yards from your tent and have no idea where it is, so attempting to continue an expedition would be foolish in the extreme.

An Arctic blizzard can be a completely disorientating "whiteout," and there is no option but to sit it out in your tent. If you need to go out, say to feed the sled dogs or go to the toilet, you may need to mark your route to ensure you can get back, perhaps laying out a cord to help retrace your steps. Don't rely on footprints that could soon be covered and hard to spot. Otherwise, in those immortal words, you "may be some time."

EMERGENCY SNOW SHELTERS

In a life-or-death situation the insulating powers of snow could make all the difference. There may not be time to start crafting igloos, but experienced guides or leaders can make basic snow shelters quickly enough, burrowing into a snow drift to make a snow cave or even digging down below the ground if necessary.

A snow wall was built by the Serious Arctic team to prepare for a storm coming in. The wall protected the tents from 100 km/h (60 mph) winds, but a blizzard that followed confined the adventurers to their tents for two days.

Inuit Survival

The Inuit were the first inhabitants of the Arctic, arriving over four thousand years ago. Originally living largely as nomads, many still take to the frozen land, hunting for the animals that traditionally provided all their needs from food and clothes to tools and weapons. They've developed an extraordinary range of skills to cope with such a hostile environment, and many of their techniques and inventions have been taken up in the wider world.

The Inuit were first to use dog sleds (page 40) and igloos (page 48), and also invented the kayak. Designed to use when hunting sea mammals, kayaks are lightweight, fast, and maneuverable. Covered in animal skin, usually caribou or seal, they have a small hole for the hunter to slot into. The traditional craft is remarkably watertight.

An Inuit prepares to go hunting.

 ## WHY DO the Inuit stay in such a harsh environment?

An Inuit might well ask the same question of someone living in a hot country. As the Inuit moved further north, their bodies evolved to be uniquely adapted to the cold. They have a high metabolic rate, burning fat faster than normal to produce more body heat. They're also short and stocky (average height 160 cm/5 ft 3 in), with short arms, legs, fingers, and toes. This means they have a much smaller surface area for their weight, and as most body heat is lost through the skin they are able to keep much warmer. It also means they would be quite uncomfortable in a hot climate.

Apart from the physical modifications, the Inuit also feel they have a spiritual connection with their spectacular frozen world. Even though most no longer live permanently out on the land, hunting is a strong part of their tradition, and they would be very reluctant to give it up.

An Inuit child, dressed in traditional gear, hugs a young sled dog.

The Inuit are spread extremely thinly across the Arctic regions of Canada, Alaska, Russia, and Greenland, with a total population of around 150,000. Originally known as Eskimos by the rest of the world, they voted in 1977 for an official name change to Inuit. The different populations share similar ways of life and customs, though they speak a variety of languages.

Few Inuit follow a nomadic lifestyle anymore. Most have moved into houses in small communities, with "luxuries" like running water and central heating. While many are still involved in hunting and enjoy traditional foods and culture, there are concerns that the unique survival skills passed down over centuries will soon disappear.

WASTE NOT, WANT NOT

The Arctic has no trees and, apart from a few hardy mosses and lichens, no plants for most of the year. With animals as their only natural resource, the Inuit use great ingenuity to make sure few parts go to waste.

SEALS

Inuit tradition describes seal as a "special food," the most important part of the diet for health and warmth. Like most meat, the Inuit eat seal both cooked and uncooked. Raw seal meat will be eaten while still warm straight after the kill, or sucked and chewed on later when it's frozen (but still uncooked).

Body parts eaten include the intestine, flippers, heart, liver, tongue, brain, eyeball, blubber, and even the mustache. Seal meat is also fed to sled dogs.

Seal skins have many uses, from tents and boats to waterproof clothing and boots (mukluks), while seal fat is used as fuel for cooking and lighting.

CARIBOU (OR REINDEER)

Caribou are another major part of the diet, and again the Inuit let little go to waste, eating the heart, liver, tongue, stomach lining, and even the stomach contents.

The caribou's fur hide is an extremely warm material for clothing and is also used for mats. Bones and antlers are used for tools, and the animal's tendons are turned into sewing thread and cord.

POLAR BEARS

Both the meat and fat is eaten (but polar bear meat is never eaten raw because it contains parasites). Polar bear skins are used for rugs, and in some areas for clothing, though it is not as flexible as seal and caribou skins. Teeth and claws are used for jewelry.

BOWHEAD WHALES

As a huge, slow-swimming Arctic whale, bowheads were hunted by the Inuit for thousands of years. This had little effect on the bowhead population, but commercial whaling by the rest of the world over the last two hundred years almost wiped out the whale. Hunting was banned in the late twentieth century, and the Inuit are now allowed to take only a tiny number.

The bowhead whale is a prized source of food and much else besides, with one animal supplying an entire Inuit community for months. The blubber is used both as food and as oil for heat and light. The huge jaw and rib bones are used to make everything from roof supports to runners for sleds, while the massive baleen (whalebone) plates found in the whale's mouth make frames for kayaks, tools, and other equipment.

Other types of whale are also much sought after. A special delicacy is the skin and thin blubber layer of belugas and narwhals, which are known as muktuk.

ARCTIC CHAR

Often eaten raw and frozen, this fish tastes like salmon and forms another key part of the Inuit diet. The fish bones are used to make sewing needles.

HOW DO the Inuit stay healthy eating no fruit and vegetables?

One of the main things fruit and vegetables provide is vitamin C. Without it you get a disease called scurvy, which is fatal if untreated. This used to be common among sailors who went on long journeys without access to fresh fruit and vegetables.

The Inuit have several alternative sources in their diet. In particular, whale skin and blubber—muktuk—is rich in vitamin C (but has traditionally not been eaten by westerners including, ironically, commercial whalers who often fell victim to scurvy). The stomach contents of caribou are another source of the vitamin, though again this delicacy is not to the taste of many outside the Inuit community. Small amounts of vitamin C in other meat and fish are largely lost when food is cooked, so it also helps that the Inuit eat much of it raw.

WE'RE GOING ON A BEAR HUNT...

As polar bears are now an endangered species, hunting is banned worldwide. However, because of their traditional reliance on the animal, Inuit communities are allowed a small, tightly controlled quota to kill.

Controversially they often encourage big-game sports hunters to come and take part in the kills. The Inuit argue that the polar bears are going to be killed anyway and it brings in much-needed cash (around $34,000 per animal), but some animal campaigners are against the practice, believing it cruel and unnecessary.

Serious

── IT'S A JUNGLE OUT THERE

Whether it's swinging through the trees like Tarzan, avoiding the snakes coiled on every branch, or slashing through the dense undergrowth with a machete, we all grow up with strong images of the jungle. Most of these come from stories and films, and they provide a very misleading impression of day-to-day life in the jungle—to the extent that on arrival in a real rainforest the first reaction may well be one of slight disappointment. A lot of jungle is not that dense, looking much like a forest back home (though with much taller and impressive trees), and at first glance there may appear to be very little wildlife.

Over time, however, the richness and magic of the rainforest slowly starts to come through. The constant wall of sound is extraordinary and electrifying, evidence that the rainforest is actually

Jungle

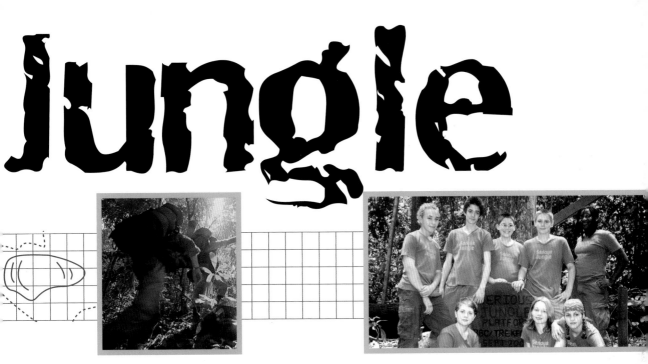

teeming with a breathtaking range of creatures. Many of them will try to avoid you—a rare sighting of a snake is to be treasured, though it is usually just a glimpse as it slithers off as fast as it can.

But the difficulty of living in the jungle is something the movies have got right. You will be covered in mud, bathed in sweat, bitten by mosquitoes, soaked in tropical downpours, and probably have leeches in unmentionable places. And, in the midst of it all, you will also hopefully have one of the most memorable adventures of your life.

RAINFOREST DEVASTATION

Humans are decimating the world's rainforests in just "the blink of an eye" in terms of the history of the Earth. Tropical hardwood trees like mahogany and teak are in great demand in developed countries like the United States, UK, and Japan. The beautiful, hard-wearing wood from a single mahogany tree can fetch around $85,000. Once valuable trees are taken out, forests are also cleared (slashed and burned) for farmland.

It's estimated that tropical rainforests are being destroyed at an alarming rate—around 250 sq km (100 sq miles) every day. Given that the total remaining area is roughly 8,000,000 sq km (3,000,000 sq miles), it means we'll have wiped out the rainforests before the end of this century if nothing changes. Depressingly, at the moment it's hard to see what is going to halt this. Despite token attempts to control illegal logging, the insatiable demand for hardwood combined with the forces of big business and corrupt governments in rainforest countries appear completely unstoppable.

The World's Rainforests

Greenland

Siberia

NORTH

AMERICA

EUROPE

ASIA

Tropic of Cancer

Atlantic
Ocean

AFRICA

SOUTH EAST
ASIA

Pacific
Ocean

Equator

Congo Basin

Amazon

SOUTH
AMERICA

Indian
Ocean

Tropic of Capricorn

AUSTRALIA

Pacific
Ocean

Southern
Ocean

The World's Rainforests

tropical rainforest

edge of rainforest undergoing
the most rapid deforestation

ANTARCTICA

Rainforests stretch round the globe's tropical regions near
the equator. By far the largest is the Amazon (see page 182),
accounting for half of the world's tropical rainforest, with
much of the rest in the Congo Basin and Southeast Asia. In
all, rainforests cover about 5 percent of the world's land
surface, roughly the area of Australia.

WHY ARE rainforests so important?

Many reasons. Here are just some of them:

- Although they take up just one-twentieth of the Earth's land, it's estimated that tropical rainforests are home to around half of all types of animals and plants. Many of these remain to be discovered and analyzed, but at the present rate of destruction may be gone before we get the chance.

- Many medicines come from the rainforest, so we could also be destroying unique, priceless cures for diseases.

- Rainforests help recycle the air we breathe, taking in carbon dioxide and giving out oxygen (the opposite of human lungs) during the process of photosynthesis, in which leaves convert sunlight into energy. The Amazon is often called "the lungs of the Earth" for this reason, though the importance of the recycling effect is disputed (some scientists say it is insignificant compared to the global role played by oceans in absorbing CO_2 and producing oxygen).

- Rainforests have a great effect on the world's climate and the regions around them. As the forest disappears, surrounding areas may experience devastating changes in their weather.

- Many different tribespeople have lived in harmony with nature in the rainforest for generations, relying on the forest for all their needs. Unfortunately, most tribes are now disappearing rapidly (see page 208).

The Serious Jungle Adventure

The Serious Jungle eight flew halfway round the world to the island of Borneo in Southeast Asia on an environmental mission to help endangered orangutans. As they got off the plane, they felt as if they'd walked straight into a sauna. The heat and humidity was more extreme than any of them had imagined. Simply carrying their backpacks left them exhausted and bathed in sweat, and at this stage the idea of working round the clock in the jungle seemed an impossibility. As one of the young adventurers commented: "I'll never complain about the British weather again!"

Fifteen hours of flying and an eight-hour time difference certainly didn't help, and the team were given a few days based just outside the rainforest to acclimatize and take part in jungle training.

One of the boys unfortunately had a phobia of spiders, and in particular had an irrational fear he would swallow a tarantula while he was asleep. So he came up with an ingenious (if pointless) solution. Before getting into bed he used the eyeshield issued on the aircraft to cover his mouth.

Next morning the team visited the renowned Sepilok Orangutan Rehabilitation Centre and met the remarkable endangered creatures they had come to help. Most of the young orangutans here are orphans that were taken illegally from the wild as pets, before being rescued by the Centre.

The ambitious Serious Jungle mission

Orphaned babies have to be bottlefed every few hours (above).

—WHY DOES IT rain so much in a rainforest?

As the name suggests, rainforests are some of the wettest places on earth, getting about 200-1,000 cm (80-400 in) of rainfall each year. If it all fell at once, 200 cm (80 in) would submerge an adult human, and 1,000 cm (400 in) would cover their house too.

So where does all the rain come from? If you've been on vacation in the tropics, you'll probably have experienced rain and thunderstorms, especially in the afternoon.

This is because the powerful, tropical sun directly overhead causes great evaporation from the ocean, and as the day wears on the clouds often build up over land. This pattern also affects tropical rainforests, and in addition the forests provide a lot of their own rain—the heat of the sun causes moisture from leaves to evaporate, again leading to a build up of rain clouds. When it's not actually raining, the forest is usually incredibly humid.

was to build a huge feeding platform in the heart of the jungle, the last stage in returning the captive orangutans to the wild (see page 80). Some of the youngest animals were in diapers, and with their incredibly human-like features, especially the ears, fingers, and tiny nails, the adventurers found them completely enchanting. As with human babies, there was an endless round of jobs to be done, and the team helped with weighing, bathing, and bottlefeeding the orangutans.

Two days into training, the adventurers spent their first night in the rainforest. It was a gentle introduction to jungle life, with a trek of little more than an hour on well-worn paths, not a drop of rain, and the knowledge that they'd be back in relative civilization within twenty-four hours. Nevertheless, most of the team were quite traumatized by the experience—not least because of a series of animal encounters, which included leeches, mosquitoes, and a scorpion just underneath one of the sleeping sites.

Homesickness swept through the camp, and by the time it came to tucking up inside their hammocks, with the incessant sound of creatures all around in the darkness, several adventurers were feeling very vulnerable, scared, and alone.

But first light in the jungle is a magical time, and a good night's sleep had worked wonders for the exhausted team. Spirits were much higher knowing they had survived the night and were heading back out.

Some rainforests have no dry and wet seasons. Rain just pours down throughout the year. But August in this corner of Borneo is reckoned to be relatively dry, so much so that the main worry in planning the trip was to ensure that there would be enough water to drink once in the jungle. Throughout jungle training there had been almost no rain but, as if on cue, the heavens opened just as the team were packing to start the main expedition. It was an ominous sign of what was to come.

They headed downriver by powerboat, leaving them a two-day trek into the rainforest to get to their main campsite where they would spend the rest of the expedition building the feeding platform.

It's a common misconception that rainforests are flat. In fact, they're often very hilly, and the

Building the Serious Jungle feeding platform in the heart of the Borneo rainforest.

adventurers made slow progress in extremely difficult terrain. They went up a treacherous, muddy slope to meet an equally steep one down the other side, followed by wading across a snake-infested stream and more steep slopes to tackle. Hours of work went into covering a distance of perhaps just 100 m (330 ft) as the "crow" flies, and all in temperatures of around 30°C (86°F) plus extreme humidity.

After seven hours of hiking, the team called a halt for the day but still had to make camp. This meant putting up hammocks, gathering firewood, washing in a nearby stream, gathering and purifying water, and making supper. As if that wasn't enough, an orangutan had started to take an interest in the group. Stalking them from the trees, it was threatening to take any backpack or piece of kit left unattended. The animal then literally "peed down" as it urinated exactly where one adventurer was trying to put up his hammock.

The leeches were also starting to bug some of the adventurers. Although the blood-sucking worms are pretty harmless, one girl was quite freaked out to find a leech in a rather personal place after she'd been to the toilet.

A further day of hiking finally brought them to their jungle base, and the team were much happier in the knowledge they could settle at last and make it home for the next ten days.

Each day there would still be a half-hour trek up and down slippery slopes to get to and from the building site, loaded up with helmets, harnesses, and tools. The camp had to be situated near a flowing stream to provide drinking water.

The project—a huge 3 m (10 ft) square hardwood feeding platform, positioned 6m (20 ft) up a tree—was massive. The adventurers had two local carpenters to give advice, but it was still a daunting prospect, especially when on the first day they were hit by a full tropical downpour. If the journey to the building site was tricky, the trek back was close to impossible, slithering down mud banks cascading with water. Along the way, the team had to cross several streams by walking across fallen logs, and in the pouring rain one adventurer slipped and fell in. He was none the worse for wear, but soon after felt something sharp wriggling around in his groin area. On further

Ropes are strung between feeding platforms at the Sepilok Rehabilitation Centre to encourage orangutans to head into the forest.

investigation, a black crab leapt out of his pants.

This was the rainforest living up to its name, with constant heavy rain turning the camp into a quagmire, and all personal gear soaked and covered in mud. It was hard to believe there had been genuine concerns about getting enough water. The dangers of the environment really hit home when a tree crashed to the ground just yards away from the adventurers.

With the bad weather slowing down building, a bizarre incident put them even further behind schedule. As the feeding platform was being built, a small camera had been placed at the top of the tree to film the construction from above. When the expedition leader, Bruce Parry, made one of his regular climbs up the tree to change batteries and tapes he made a worrying discovery. An orangutan had stolen the camera and was waving it around just a few yards away. If dropped by the animal it could have been a lethal weapon, so the site had to be cleared. Bits of the camera started raining down as the orangutan took it to pieces, including a tape cassette that it had ejected and unspooled. The film crew later managed to repair the tape—which showed the very moment the orangutan took the camera!

Next morning, Bruce found the remains of the camera balanced precariously between two branches. Once he had removed it, the building work was at last able to continue.

The eight adventurers completed the platform in ten days—a hugely impressive achievement. A group of young orangutans were brought along to try it out and took to the platform immediately, an emotional moment for all the team. The animals would now live in the area around the platform, fed for as long as needed till eventually they returned completely to the wild.

A group of young orangutans have their first feed at the Serious Jungle platform.

EXPEDITION LOCATION

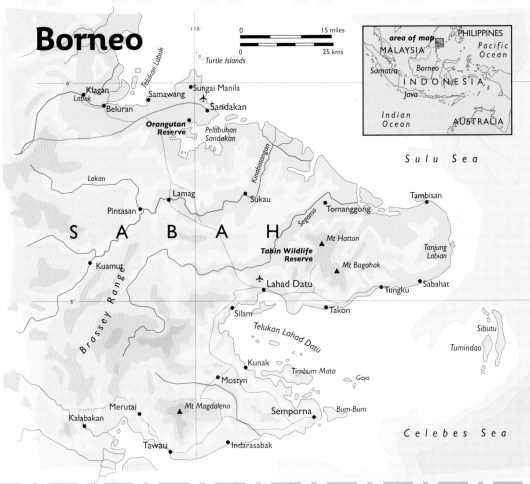

Borneo

118°

0 ——— 15 miles
0 ——— 25 kms

area of map
PHILIPPINES
MALAYSIA
Pacific Ocean
Sumatra
Borneo
INDONESIA
Java
Indian Ocean
AUSTRALIA

Turtle Islands

6°
Klagan
Labuk
Beluran
Telukan Labuk
Samawang
Sungai Manila
Sandakan
Orangutan Reserve
Pelabuhan Sandakan

Sulu Sea

Lokan
Lamag
Pintasan
Sukau
Kinabatangan
Tambisan
Segama
Tomanggong

S A B A H

▲ Mt Hatton
Tabin Wildlife Reserve
▲ Mt Bagahak
Tanjung Labian

Kuamut
Brassey Range
Lahad Datu
Tungku
Sabahat

5°
Silam
Takon

Sibutu
Tumindao

Telukan Lahad Datu
Kunak
Timbum Mata
Gaya

Mostyn
▲ *Mt Magdaleno*
Semporna
Bum-Bum

Kalabakan
Merutai

Tawau
Indarasabak

Celebes Sea

The Serious Jungle team was in a small pocket of rainforest near the east coast of Sabah in Malaysian Borneo.

THE ISLAND OF BORNEO

Sitting directly on the equator, Borneo is one of the biggest islands in the world. The majority of the island, known as Kalimantan, is part of Indonesia, while the northern provinces of Sarawak and Sabah are part of Malaysia. The tiny country of Brunei is on the north coast.

Mention of the name Borneo conjures up primeval, inaccessible forest cut off from the modern world, and until recent times that was certainly true. Covered in dense rainforest with trees up to 60 m (200 ft) tall, rivers were the only way of traveling into the interior, and most became impassable a few miles inland.

But Borneo has been comprehensively logged, slashed, and burnt in the past thirty years. Huge forest fires raged out of control for months in 1997 and 1998. Started deliberately, they blanketed the island in thick, acrid smoke and destroyed vast areas of rainforest.

Now the rainforest is a shadow of its former self, covering only half the island and still shrinking rapidly. Although the heart of Borneo still contains mystical, unexplored areas, these are not expected to survive more than a few decades unless drastic action is taken.

The young adventurers built the huge hardwood platform at a height of 6 m (20 ft).

THE ALARMING EXTENT OF BORNEO DEFORESTATION

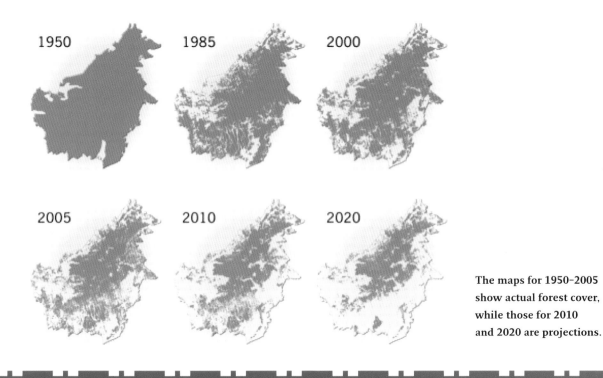

1950 1985 2000

2005 2010 2020

The maps for 1950–2005 show actual forest cover, while those for 2010 and 2020 are projections.

As these maps show, Borneo has sufffered from severe deforestation over the last thirty years, with more destruction set to follow during the next decade or so.

Borneo Wildlife

The Borneo jungle is a unique, extraordinary habitat teeming with unique animal life. It also has the unfortunate distinction of being perhaps the most devastated rainforest in the history of the planet. Borneo is home to an incredible range of creatures, many of which are now critically endangered. Just in the last decade, scientists have discovered about four hundred new species on the island.

The Borneo rainforest has around three hundred known types of mammal alone, of which around one hundred are types of bat. A handful of the key threatened mammals are mentioned here (for some of the more dangerous creatures, see page 82).

ORANGUTAN

Found only in Borneo and the neighboring island of Sumatra, the highly intelligent orangutan is one of the great apes—humans' closest relatives along with chimpanzees and gorillas. The name orangutan has nothing to do with the fact that the animal has orangey-brown hair. It actually means "person of the forest" in Malaysian.

Orangutans are the largest tree-dwelling animals in the world. They spend almost all their time up in the trees, using their immensely powerful arms and hands to swing effortlessly from branch to branch. Each night they make a platform to sleep on high up in the trees, bending or breaking off branches and adding leaves and twigs. They may even add a roof of leaves to keep out the rain.

Orangutans eat mainly fruit, and display an amazing knowledge of when different rainforest trees are about to bear fruit, which may be only once every few years.

Orangutans give birth only around every eight years, the longest interval of any mammal.

Orangutans are completely at home in the trees.

Offspring are carried around for the first five years and stay with their mothers until the next baby comes along.

Just twenty years ago there were thought to be around one hundred thousand orangutans in the wild. Now their numbers are plummeting, with recent estimates suggesting well under fifty thousand remaining.

BORNEO RHINO

All but extinct this is a subspecies of the critically endangered Sumatran rhino (found only on the neighboring island of Sumatra and on the Malaysian mainland). Living in the most remote, dense rainforest, it is hard to estimate remaining numbers, but there are thought to be as few as just twenty-five left, probably too few for the population to survive in the long term. As with its Sumatran cousin, rainforest destruction and poaching for its "valuable" horn and other body parts are the main threats. The rarely-seen animal was only caught on camera for the first time in 2006 by a remotely triggered camera trap.

A proboscis monkey
displays its fleshy nose.

The Sumatran rhino pictured left is critically endangered. Its even rarer Borneo cousin has hardly ever been caught on camera.

PROBOSCIS MONKEY

This endangered monkey is only found in Borneo and is, needless to say, best known for its huge fleshy nose (or proboscis), which droops right down to its chin.

The function of the long nose is not known. But, as only the male has this distinctive feature, it may be that it's evolved as a sign of fertility and strength for breeding (however unappealing to the human eye).

Living in the trees by rivers and in mangrove swamps, proboscis monkeys are good swimmers. They will also wade through the water on two feet like humans.

BORNEO ELEPHANT

Borneo pygmy elephants are only found in the northeast corner of the island and are closely related to the Asian elephant, though recent DNA studies suggest they are a separate subspecies that evolved on the island thousands of years ago. They are smaller than Asian elephants and have tails so long they may even drag on the ground. They are the true kings of the jungle, with no predators other than humans. Once again, deforestation is the main threat, and there are now thought to be just a few thousand remaining.

CLOUDED LEOPARD

As with the Borneo elephant, the clouded leopard found in Borneo (and Sumatra) has recently been identified as a different species to the clouded leopards elsewhere in Asia. This highly endangered cat takes its name from the beautiful, cloud-like patterns on its skin. The Borneo species is darker in color with smaller markings than its cousins on the mainland.

The clouded leopard's body is around a yard in length with a tail almost as long. The rare cat is so elusive that most of what is known about its behavior comes from observing it in captivity. It is an excellent tree climber, able to descend a tree trunk head first. Using its sharp claws it can even travel upside-down along a branch. Gibbons and proboscis monkeys are among its prey. Habitat destruction and poaching for body parts for use in Chinese medicine are the main threats. Estimates suggest ten to twenty thousand may remain in Borneo and Sumatra.

SUN BEAR

Also known as the honey bear or dog bear, this endangered animal is the smallest of the eight bear species. Adult males weigh only around 65 kg (140 lbs), less than most adult humans, and are just three to four feet in length. Even so, they are probably the most aggressive of all bears, sometimes attacking even if unprovoked.

The name sun bear comes from the distinctive orangey-yellow crescent on the chest, which is said to resemble the rising sun. The animals are mainly nocturnal and are good tree climbers. They use their long tongues to take honey from beehives. Again, forest destruction and use in Chinese medicine are the main threats.

–THREATS TO ORANGUTANS

A whole host of different factors have combined to leave the orangutan critically endangered:

- **The most devastating has been the destruction of vast areas of their habitat, the lowland rainforest.**
- **Forest fires that are started deliberately each year to clear land have killed thousands (relatively few animals die in the fires themselves, but by losing their forest home).**
- **Orangutans are quite solitary and need a large area of jungle as their "home range." Even if pockets of rainforest survive, they may be too small to support orangutan populations.**
- **Many young orangutans are taken illegally for the pet trade. Mothers are often killed by the poachers—and sometimes eaten as "bushmeat."**

- **Orangutans wandering onto farmland are seen as pests by farmers (who again often shoot them for "bushmeat").**
- **As female orangutans have only around three babies at most in their lives, it is hard for populations to recover.**

Huge areas of Borneo's rainforest have been cleared for palm oil plantations.

THE ORANGUTAN PROJECT

The Sepilok Orangutan Rehabilitation Centre is one of Malaysia's leading centers for returning orangutans to the wild. The Centre has successfully reintroduced more than one hundred animals in the last forty years, mainly orphaned orangutans rescued from the pet trade.

Training the animals for life in the wild is a long process, taking around six years. For the first three years the orphaned orangutans live in a nursery, where the wardens encourage them to develop basic skills like swinging from ropes. At age three, the animals are led daily into the rainforest to feed. Using ropes strung between feeding platforms, they're gradually persuaded to travel further from the nursery.

By age five or six, the orangutans will usually stay out in the rainforest overnight, and the wardens gradually reduce the amount of food brought to the last feeding platform, with the aim that the orangutans will begin to forage for their own food and eventually not come back to the platform at all.

The new feeding platform that the Centre asked Serious Jungle to build deep in the jungle was designed to help with the last step in the reintroduction process.

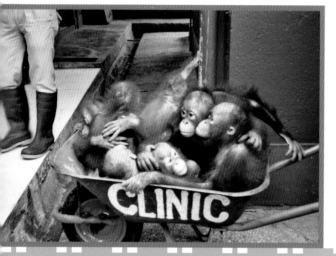

Young orphans at the Sepilok Orangutan Centre are wheeled off every few days for weighing and washing.

CAN YOU hug an orangutan?

Very tempting, but not to be recommended for all sorts of reasons, not least that it might just hug you back and crush you with its hugely powerful arms. An adult male weighs up to twice an average adult human, and the strength required to support itself swinging in the trees is phenomenal. It can be quite territorial and aggressive towards humans.

The babies are, of course, incredibly cute (the root of their problem in being taken as pets). Orphans will naturally adopt you and wrap their long arms round you like a human baby, but if they're to be reintroduced to the wild they should have as little human contact as possible.

Orangutans are clever and very mischievous. They quickly learn to "ape" human skills, for example, undoing buttons and zips. The Serious Jungle adventurers and crew had to watch out constantly when filming around the Rehabilitation Centre. If any item like a camera was left loose in a pocket or even in a zipped-up bag, little orangutan fingers would soon be inside and the animal would be off with its prize in seconds.

Dangerous Creatures

Snakes, scorpions, spiders, tarantulas, leeches, centipedes . . . the endless list of creepy-crawlies and dangerous creatures found in the jungle is enough to send shivers down the spine. Many people have a real phobia of at least one of them, but while nearly all these creatures are potentially dangerous, most are absolutely not out to get you. Taking the right precautions means the risks are actually very low, and with time you will hopefully come to appreciate what beautiful creatures they are (with the possible exception of those slug-like, blood-sucking leeches—definitely not for the squeamish).

HOW TO AVOID DANGEROUS CREATURES

Like most animals, the vast majority of potentially dangerous jungle inhabitants are not at all aggressive towards humans, only attacking if cornered or threatened.

In the unlikely event you encounter a large mammal, such as a monkey or orangutan, you are very unlikely to have a problem as long as you back away slowly.

The smaller creatures are actually much more of a danger, not least because it's much easier to threaten them by accident. But there are various precautions you can take in order to reduce the risk of this happening:

- Keep all bags and backpacks sealed at all times. Don't reach in blindly—check where your hand is going in case something has snuck in. One Serious adventurer unzipped his wash-bag in the dark and reached in to grab his toothbrush, only to recoil as he felt something wriggling.

Closer inspection with a flashlight revealed that a huge cockroach had squeezed in through a gap where the zipper wasn't fully zipped.

- When walking into undergrowth, stepping on a snake is the last thing you want to do (it may just *be* the last thing you actually do), so stamp your feet and rustle around to let snakes and other creatures know you're coming. They will be off like a shot.
- Always wear sturdy boots when walking around. If you do accidentally step on a snake, its bite will probably not penetrate the boot.
- Put boots upside down on sticks overnight to discourage things from crawling in. Then hit them together to get anything out before putting your feet in.
- Watch where you're sitting or what you're resting on, or you could end up leaning against a camouflaged tarantula or other creepy-crawly.

WHAT'S THE most dangerous thing in the rainforest?

Perhaps surprisingly, none of the creatures mentioned here are the most dangerous. While some of them can deliver a deadly bite, incidents are relatively rare. Those who travel regularly in the rainforest know there are other dangers that present much greater risks as they affect many more people. The top five are probably the following:

- Mosquitoes—may carry malaria or dengue fever (see page 94).
- Unpurified water—carries a host of diseases including typhoid and cholera.
- Heat exhaustion—can hit you very quickly and if not treated leads to heatstroke, which can be fatal (see page 93).
- Deadfall—as the name suggests, this is dead trees or branches falling to the ground. As you might expect in a rainforest, deadfall is a common occurrence.
- Getting lost—incredibly easy to do. One minute you're happily wandering along with your expedition, the next you're alone and in a nightmarish situation (see page 99).

- Be careful where you put your hand when grabbing onto tree trunks and branches as you walk through the forest, especially in difficult terrain where you might reach out suddenly to steady yourself.
- Keep your sleeping bag zipped up and inside your mosquito net during the day (see page 108). Check it before getting in.
- Always wear long-sleeved shirts and consider tucking your pants into your boots.
- Never leave food lying around in camp.

SNAKES

To say snakes get a bad press is an understatement. Mere mention of these limbless reptiles strikes fear into many, but they are quite remarkable, fascinating creatures, often with striking patterns on their scaly skin, which is quite dry to the touch, not slimy as some believe. Most are not dangerous. Of around three thousand known species, only about ten percent are venomous, and of those, just a tiny handful would ever attack a human without provocation.

MY NEXT TRICK IS IMPOSSIBLE

The jaws of snakes are able to "unhinge," allowing them to eat things bigger than their own head. All snakes are meat eaters, catching insects, worms, birds, and small mammals like mice and rats. Larger species can swallow chickens or rabbits whole, and the huge reticulated python, found in Borneo, has been known to swallow an entire pig or small deer. It's one of the world's longest snakes, growing up to 10 m (33 ft). Known as a constrictor, the huge python kills its prey by coiling itself around and squeezing tightly to constrict breathing (contrary to popular belief, constrictors don't actually crush their victims).

This may understandably make you wonder what you would do if you found yourself with a reticulated python wrapped around you. Some suggest that in this event you should simply pick an end and start uncoiling it. Whether you would have the strength to do this is highly debatable, but the situation is frankly so rare that it's not worth worrying about. While humans have been killed by reticulated pythons, it's usually owners of pet pythons who've put themselves in extremely dangerous situations.

DEALING WITH A SNAKE BITE

If you have been bitten it may be difficult at first to know how serious the situation is. Even if you get a good look at the snake, which is unlikely, it is tricky for all but an expert to identify it accurately. To confuse things further, many quite harmless snakes mimic the markings and colorings of their lethal relatives. Until proved otherwise, you should always assume the worst and take action as if you've had a large dose of venom.

It is one of those impossible times when you have to try to stay very calm. Frantic activity will only increase the speed at which the poison travels round your body.

Snake venoms act in different ways to incapacitate the victim. They may affect the nervous system, bring on internal bleeding, act directly on the heart, or cause severe swelling and tissue damage around the area of the bite. There is much misinformation about treating snake bites.

The key things to AVOID are:

- Tying tight tourniquets around arms or legs (these will completely cut off the blood supply to your limbs, causing great damage).
- Making deep cuts around the bite area (which will just allow more venom into your bloodstream).
- Sucking out the venom into your mouth (this may look macho but is pretty ineffective).
- Carrying antivenom and injecting it at the site of the incident, unless expert local medics advise otherwise (most antivenom needs to be refrigerated, and giving the wrong antivenom could seriously worsen your condition).

What you should DO is:

- Get to hospital as soon as possible. Hopefully the expedition will have identified in advance a hospital with antivenom and drawn up an evacuation plan to ensure it can be reached in a maximum of four hours. (It's comforting to note that in the majority of cases so little venom has been injected that the hospital

CAN YOU die if you get bitten by a snake?

It is certainly possible, but it is far more unlikely than films and folklore might lead you to think. While most snakes can deliver a bit of a bite, few are venomous. Those that are have hollow fangs and inject the venom down the middle of them, but even the most lethal snakes will rarely inject a full dose. You are not a meal for them and it would take them days to "recharge" their venom glands to go after real prey.

Another movie myth is that snake bites kill humans in minutes. This is extremely rare, and would probably only occur if an exceptional set of circumstances combined, for example, a full dose of venom from an extremely toxic snake injected into a very young child or frail elderly person. In general, if you take the right action you will have several hours before things start to become critical.

decides not to actually use antivenom).

- Keep the bite area lower than the heart and try to move as little as possible.
- Wrap a pressure bandage round an arm or leg a little above the bite, continuing down over the wound. This may help slow down the spread of the venom, but it must be loose enough not to cut off the circulation completely. A good measure is whether you can still slide a finger under it.
- Avoid eating or drinking anything.
- If possible—which is rarely the case—kill the snake to bring for identification. This is one for an experienced guide only, and should not divert attention at all from getting quickly to the hospital. (Special suction devices are available to draw out the venom, but as it's reckoned they get out less than half of it at best, the sensible plan may again be to concentrate on getting to medical help.)

BORNEO'S VENOMOUS SNAKES

Some of the key venomous snakes found in Borneo include:

- Russell's viper—around 1–1.5 m (3–5 ft) in length and said to be responsible for more deaths in the area than any other snake. Coils up and hisses when threatened and strikes very fast. Its venom causes blood to clot and severe swelling of the bite area.
- Green tree pit viper—a small, green viper of around 50 cm (20 in) in length. Its venom is much less dangerous than its larger relative, but the snake is notable as it lives almost permanently in the trees and can inflict severe bites on the head, neck and shoulders. Pit vipers are able to track down and bite their prey in complete darkness. Two holes near the eyes (the pits which give the snake its name) can "see" the infrared rays given off by anything warm, including potential victims.
- The common cobra—up to 2 m (6 ft) in length. Lifts up its head and spreads its hood when alarmed. The tactic is designed to scare its enemies, and it's certainly chilling to witness. Bites can be very serious, affecting the nervous system and causing difficulty breathing.

SCORPIONS

This is another creature whose reputation is worse than its "bite." Scorpions are members of the spider family (arachnids) with eight legs, plus two sharp pincers like a lobster. There are well over a thousand types of scorpion, ranging in size from just over 1 cm (0.5 in) to 18 cm (7 in). Few of these species could possibly kill a human, and a healthy adult would almost always survive.

The sting is, of course, in the tail, which is often arched over forwards in trademark fashion. The venom is injected though the stinger at the end, and as a rule of thumb the smaller the type of scorpion the more dangerous its sting. This is probably to compensate for its small pincers when capturing prey.

Often the effect is no worse than a bee sting, but local experts will be only too aware if there are any particularly lethal types of scorpion in the area. If stung by one of these, follow similar steps as for snake bites and get to hospital, where antivenom should be available.

Scorpions are largely nocturnal, and head for enclosed, dark areas such as backpacks and boots. The Serious Jungle team found countless scorpions hidden in the piles of wood they were using for their building project. If you have to pick up wood, stones, or bricks, wear thick gloves and perform your task with great caution.

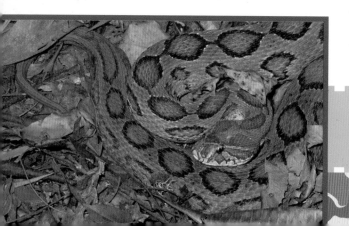

The deadly Russell's viper is found across South Asia from India to Borneo.

SPIDERS AND TARANTULAS

Arachnophobia, the fear of spiders, is widespread, though if you've ever watched the quite unbelievable skill with which a spider spins silk and delicately weaves a web it's hard to understand why. As ever, literature has a lot to answer for, as few spiders and tarantulas are harmful and it is extremely rare for one to kill a healthy human. The bites of most venomous spiders will just cause swelling around the wound, but local knowledge of types of spider will help you decide if you should go to hospital where, if necessary, antivenom should be available.

If it's possible to catch or kill the offending spider safely, bring it along with you to help with identification.

 - # TARANTULA or spider?

Tarantulas are particularly hairy members of the spider family, and are often bigger than other spiders. Although they are portrayed as especially scary, they are surprisingly delicate and no more dangerous than other spiders. (They are also actually rather tasty—see page 203.)

CENTIPEDES, MILLIPEDES, AND CATERPILLARS

The phrase "creepy-crawly" could have been designed for these guys. Many are harmless but there are some types that can be dangerous to humans. Local guides should be able to tell you which species are safe to handle. If you are in any doubt, though, give them a wide berth.

- Centipedes have flattened bodies divided into anything from around fifteen to a hundred and eighty segments. Each segment has a pair of legs. (The name centipede means "hundred feet" in Latin, but some will have rather fewer and some many more.) They have venomous claws just behind the head, and some of the thousands of species can cause pain and swelling in humans.

- Millipedes have oval-shaped bodies and a similar number of segments to centipedes, but with two pairs of legs on most segments. They don't appear to quite live up to their name, which translates as "thousand legs." The maximum counted to date is around seven hundred and fifty. There are thousands of species and many will curl up into a tight ball if threatened. Some types secrete a toxic liquid that can be very irritating to the skin. Wash thoroughly if affected to minimize the effects.

- Caterpillars, of course, turn into butterflies and moths. The ones to watch out for are hairy caterpillars, which have hairs or spines for defence. If you brush against them the sharp ends are designed to break off and irritate your skin. Some caterpillars' hairs are connected to venom glands, so they may also deposit a toxic substance, which will sting and cause swelling. You may need to delicately remove the sharp ends before washing the area. If you find a caterpillar on you, simply brush it off with a twig in the direction it's crawling.

BEES AND WASPS

"Stirring up a hornet's nest" really is bad news. Swarming bees and wasps are actually among the most common dangers in a jungle. While they aren't generally aggressive towards humans, the insects will not be best pleased if you accidentally disturb their nest and they may quickly go into the attack. Individual stings are not deadly, but hundreds have been known to kill.

If a swarm attacks the expedition your guide or leader should take control and issue instructions. This is a time to move fast, covering your head if possible as you go. If by some chance you are close to buildings or tents get inside as quickly as possible, otherwise head for tall grass or bushes. You may be chased for some way, but the insects will eventually give up. Some recommend jumping into water, but swarms have been known to hover and wait for victims to surface.

In general, never swat wildly at bees or wasps because they will feel threatened and be much more likely to sting you.

If stung it's worth getting out the barbs as soon as you are clear of danger, as they continue to inject venom for several minutes. Don't pull them out with fingers or tweezers as this will just inject more venom. Instead, rake a blunt knife or fingernail across the skin to scrape them off.

A common allergic reaction to stings is anaphylactic shock, which may be extremely serious and need urgent action.

ANAPHYLACTIC SHOCK

Bites or stings may bring on an extreme allergic reaction, known as anaphylactic shock, which can be fatal in some cases if not treated quickly. One of the first symptoms is often a narrowing of the airway, which makes it hard to breathe. Those who

Although most are harmless, many-legged creepy-crawlies are best avoided—just in case!

know they are prone to the condition carry an "epi-pen." This contains the hormone adrenalin (also known as epinephrine), which, when injected into the victim, reopens the airway by reducing the swelling of the throat. Medical evacuation to hospital will also be necessary as there is risk of a further delayed reaction.

BEE OR WASP?

Bees are generally rounder and fatter than wasps and are not aggressive to humans. They feed on nectar and pollen from plants and some types make honey to help them survive the winter. Bees will only sting big mammals like humans as a last resort, as the barbed stinger remains in our relatively thick skin (along with the venom sac) and the bee then dies.

Wasps are carnivores, and eat small insects and meat, so they are much more interested in the food on your plate than bees are. They can be more aggressive than bees and have smooth stingers capable of reuse on all animals.

Hornets are types of large wasp.

BLOOD SUCKERS

Some leeches and most female mosquitoes feed on blood, which is not in itself particularly dangerous—you have plenty to share. Mosquitoes are a serious threat as they carry disease (see page 94); their bites are also very itchy. Leeches, however, are pretty harmless, and are really just included in this section because of their undoubted "yuck" factor. They have two suckers, one at each end to attach themselves, and their saliva contains a fiendish mix of chemicals to aid

feeding, including:
- An anticoagulant to stop the blood clotting
- A chemical to dilate blood vessels to maximize the blood supply
- An anaesthetic to numb the area around the wound so you don't notice it's there.

In fact leeches are so supremely good at their job that they are bred for use in modern medicine. For example, when fingers or other body parts are sewn back on after an accident, leeches may be used to keep the blood flowing into the re-attached body part.

HOW DO YOU GET LEECHES OFF YOUR BODY?

If you spend any period of time in a leech-ridden rainforest, then you may as well get used to the fact that you're going to be "leeched" sooner or later. But fear not—it's pretty painless and usually completely harmless. Some Serious Jungle adventurers even began to see it as a badge of honor: "Yeh, those leeches, to be honest I couldn't even be bothered to get them off. I knew they'd drop off when they were full."

Leeches like to come out to eat after heavy rain, and will hang from branches and leaves waiting for their next meal to walk by. They'll then drop straight onto you, or arch along the ground from sucker to sucker until they can attach themselves to your flesh (quite a creepy sight).

Because of the anaesthetic they produce, you will probably not feel a thing. If you do spot one and want to get it off, the quickest and easiest way is a quick squirt of mosquito repellent (no need for burning with cigarettes as in the movies). The possible problem with this method is that there is a slightly higher risk of infection, as the leech will regurgitate its stomach contents with the shock.

Safer is to slide your finger quickly under the small sucker near the mouth, dislodging it and making the leech stop feeding. Then do the same to the larger sucker, perhaps using your fingernail to break the suction. Finally, flick the leech away. This is great fun and games, as the leech will probably then attach to your finger, but flicking quickly with your other hand should do the trick.

The wound will bleed until the anticoagulant is flushed away, and it may also itch a little, but there should be no long-term effects apart from the general danger of infection, which applies to any wound in the jungle.

Wearing a long-sleeved shirt and a hat, and tucking pants into socks or boots will reduce the risks, but they will almost certainly find a way in eventually.

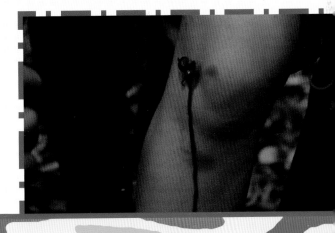

Staying Healthy

Not only is the rainforest one of the richest and most diverse environments on earth, it also has the greatest range of ways to mess you up. On top of all the dangerous creatures it's also a hotbed of tropical diseases, with other serious medical problems like heatstroke and food poisoning thrown in for good measure. Before heading to a rainforest country, you will almost certainly need to have a host of inoculations and to start a course of malaria tablets (see Preparing for the Wild, page 8). Once inside the jungle, the right precautions and routines will make the difference between a magical experience and the complete misery of feeling diabolical in the middle of nowhere.

HOT AND BOTHERED

Getting dehydrated and overheated is all too easy in the jungle, and can quickly lead to much more serious problems. It's particularly common before you've fully acclimatized to the heat.

Rainforests average 30°–34°C (86°–93°F) by day, but actually feel way hotter and stickier, with extremely high humidity levels of 75–95 percent and pretty much no wind. As you trek or work, you sweat buckets, but the high humidity prevents most of it evaporating, which is what normally produces the cooling effect on your body. Instead the sweat just soaks your clothes and drips off you while you get hotter and hotter.

You literally need to drink a small bucket-worth of water each day to keep your fluid levels up. The absolute minimum is 5 litres (1 gallon), and you'll need far more if you are very active. The best way to do this is to get into the habit of regularly sipping from a tube leading to a water-bottle in your backpack. Don't wait until you feel thirsty. You'll be absolutely amazed at how you can just keep on drinking and, incidentally, still pee no more than normal.

HEAT INDEX

Just as the wind makes the temperature feel far colder in freezing environments (see Wind chill, page 30), so the humidity makes it feel far hotter in tropical regions. This apparent temperature is known as the heat index, as shown in the chart below. For example, an air temperature of 32°C (90°F) with 90 percent humidity feels roughly like 49°C (120°F) in a non-humid environment.

HEAT INDEX CHART

The figures in the orange section of the chart represent how hot it feels at various temperatures and levels of humidity. Note that these figures are very approximate, and depend on factors like wind speed and the size of the person concerned.

TEMPERATURE (°F)

HUMIDITY	82	86	90	93	97	100
50%	82	88	93	100	109	120
60%	86	91	99	108	118	131
70%	88	95	104	117	129	145
80%	90	100	111	126	142	160
90%	93	106	120	136	156	179
100%	97	111	129	151	172	198

Why should you check the color of your pee?

Your urine is a very good indicator of whether you are getting enough fluid. A deep orangey-yellow color is bad news, suggesting you may well be dehydrated. A pale yellow or straw color is what you are aiming for. You should also be weeing more or less your normal amount, otherwise you may find yourself to be dehydrated.

TREATING HEAT EXHAUSTION AND HEATSTROKE

If you start to get a headache and feel dizzy, weak or nauseous, this is probably heat exhaustion. Muscle cramps are another sign. You should immediately stop what you're doing. Sit or lie quietly in the shade for an hour or so while sipping cool fluids (dissolving in some rehydration salts like "diarolyte" is a good idea). If possible, ask someone to fan you gently and perhaps sponge you with cool water.

If you are feeling no better after about half an hour you could be developing heatstroke, which is a medical emergency and can be fatal.

A victim of heatstroke may become confused or lose consciousness as their entire cooling system shuts down, allowing the body temperature to rise to dangerous levels of 41°C (104°F) or more. Symptoms include vomiting, a rapid, weak pulse, and rapid, shallow breathing. Evacuation to a hospital will be necessary while cooling the body as much as possible. The environment may be far from ideal for this, but if possible try to cool down areas such as the armpits, groin, and neck with cold packs or damp cloths.

Needless to say, prevention is far better than cure, so you must be absolutely rigorous about making sure you're drinking enough fluid. Check your water bottle regularly. It may reveal you've had far less than you think.

STOMACH BUGS

It's said that the one thing to spread round a jungle camp more quickly than gossip is diarrhea. The tropical rainforest is the perfect breeding ground for the bacteria, viruses, and parasites responsible for stomach bugs (gastroenteritis).

Vomiting and diarrhea away from modern conveniences in the jungle can leave you literally "feeling like death." Anyone who's experienced a bad case will never again fail to meticulously follow the rules for a vomit-free trip:

- Always wash hands in an antiseptic solution or alcohol gel after going to the toilet and before preparing food.
- Wash plates and utensils in disinfectant after meals.
- Purify any water used for drinking or cooking (see page 102).
- Store food in sealed containers.
- Cook all meat thoroughly and eat while still hot.
- Never share water bottles, plates, or cutlery.

KEEPING CLEAN

This is a very different concept to back home, as you are likely to look a complete mess most of the time wallowing in the mud with no running water and no fresh clothes. (Luckily there are few mirrors around.) However, certain areas must not be neglected. In particular:

- Each night you should wash what are euphemistically referred to as your "bits and pits," as sweating all day in the heat encourages painful rashes.
- Feet will often be soaking wet for much of the day so must be cleaned, powdered, and aired every night to avoid trench foot (so-called because it was common in the trenches in World War One). Also known as immersion foot, this is a very painful condition where the skin and nerves of the foot are damaged by being continually cold and damp. The skin begins to rot, turning white and shriveled, and often smelling awful.
- The smallest cuts and grazes (and insect bites) can quickly become infected and turn nasty in the hot, humid conditions. Apply iodine and check out regularly.
- With a buddy, inspect your body daily for leeches and other creatures like ticks.

MOSQUITOES & MALARIA

This is a classic case of the female of the species being deadlier than the male, as only female mosquitoes drink blood and therefore bite humans. The problem comes when the mosquitoes are infected with a malaria parasite, which is passed on into the human bloodstream.

There are actually four types of malaria, some more deadly than others, but with swift hospital treatment they are rarely fatal. Unfortunately, more than a million die of malaria each year in poorer countries for want of the right drugs and treatment.

No vaccine exists at the moment, so instead it's vital to take a course of malaria tablets. While they won't stop you actually getting infected they usually prevent most of the effects of the parasite. The tablets are generally taken throughout the trip, beginning before arrival and continuing for some time after returning home because malaria can take several weeks to develop.

First symptoms of malaria are often similar to very bad flu, with aching bones, chills, fever, and sweating. Cerebral malaria, which affects the brain, can quickly lead to coma and death so treatment must be given without delay.

If in doubt, assume you have malaria until

DOES MALARIA stay in your body and keep coming back?

This is a common belief as two of the four types of malaria can stay in the liver and cause fresh outbreaks over a period of years. But today there are effective drugs for killing them off completely.

proved otherwise and get medical advice as soon as possible. If you've just returned home, remember to tell the doctor you were in an exotic place, otherwise they may assume you simply have flu like the vast majority of their patients.

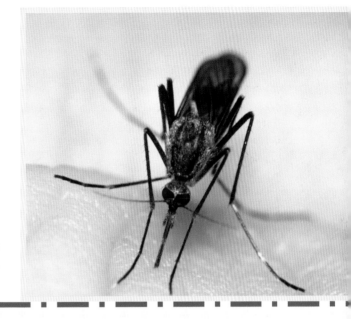

The mosquito's long proboscis pierces the skin to suck blood.

HOW CAN YOU stop mosquitoes biting you?

Not an easy one, especially when there can be so many in some areas of rainforest that they start to drive you insane. But it is definitely worth taking every precaution to minimize the chances of being bitten.

The worst times are dusk and through the night, which is when the mosquitoes feed. Always try to expose the minimum amount of flesh, wearing long-sleeved shirts and trousers, and applying an insect repellent to all exposed areas. The type of repellent is very much down to what works for you. Different concoctions seem to work better for different areas of the world, and local guides may have their favorites. The Serious expedition used 50 percent deet insect repellent on skin, and 100 percent deet on areas of clothes like collars and cuffs.

Sleep under a mosquito net, and soak it in permethrin, another repellent, at the start of the expedition. Beware of the net touching you, as mosquitoes will stick their proboscis through the netting and bite you to their heart's content.

Getting under the net in the first place is quite an art, as you want to present the smallest window of opportunity for mosquitoes to join you. (For keeping you awake, there is little to rival the high-pitched whine of a mosquito buzzing around inside the net.) A good tip is to turn off your flashlight, wait 15 seconds, and then dive in.

Some people are undoubtedly much more susceptible to mosquito bites than others. It may be particular chemicals in their sweat, so the small consolation for someone covered in itchy bites is that they probably smell particularly attractive.

Jungle Clothing

Sitting in air-conditioned civilization, it's hard to believe just how hot and sticky you will feel in a rainforest. Clothes that seem light and breezy back home may feel completely unsuitable in the jungle. In particular, cotton gets very heavy when wet and should be avoided for daytime clothing.

Jungle clothing operates on the principle of wet and dry kit, namely that you get soaked during the day, and in the evening you change into a dry set of clothes for the slightly cooler night. Since everything you bring to the rainforest has to fit inside your backpack, you may well have only one set of "wet" clothes and one set of "dry." This means that one of the more unpleasant parts of getting up in the morning is to get back into your wet kit. But hey—you'll soon be sweating like a pig anyway.

"WET" GEAR FOR DAYTIME

- Long-sleeved shirt and trousers should be light, quick-drying, but hard-wearing. Don't wear 100 percent cotton. A synthetic material like polyamide is best.
- Sunhat (for clearings and on rivers—also prevents leeches dropping into your hair).
- Sweat rag.

- Some favor "going commando" in the jungle—namely not wearing underwear—as they feel it just makes their nether regions hotter and sweatier, and so more prone to rashes. Others go to the opposite extreme, wearing lycra cycling shorts to stop leeches and insects crawling into embarrassing places.
- Boots are a source of endless debate. One side swears by jungle boots as worn by the army, the other prefers lightweight walking boots. All boots will get soaked, both in tropical downpours and as you wade through streams and bogs, so they must be able to dry out quickly. (Gore-tex is pointless in this situation). Advantages of jungle boots:
  - Dry out quickly
  - Drainage holes let out water after walking through streams
  - Can tuck in pants to avoid leeches and insects getting in

Wearing the right clothing helps you cope better with extreme conditions.

Disadvantages of jungle boots:

- Need a lot of wearing in before they become comfortable and stop giving you blisters
- Not much use back home unless you're into the military look

- Gore-tex socks are favored by some for keeping the feet dry, otherwise change into dry socks for the evening.
- Light rain jacket. This won't keep you dry (nothing will), but stops you getting cold in heavy downpours, especially if you're on the river. (It may go against the grain, but leave expensive Gore-tex jackets at home. They are ineffective in the rainforest, feel way too hot and heavy, and will quickly get trashed.)
- Belt kit or bum bag for emergency kit and extra water (see Essential Kit, page 14). All contents should be inside watertight bags.
- Backpack with fully watertight liner (see page 15).
- 3 litre (5 pint) water pouch (goes in backpack) plus drinking tube.
- Changing into shorts and T-shirt feels great, but they are impractical for trekking as you will get scratched, bitten, and "leeched." And, of course, as the sun goes down you must cover up anyway to avoid mosquito bites. Some avoid them completely, preferring the added protection of long sleeves and pants at all times.
- Work gloves are essential to avoid scorpions and other dangerous creatures when collecting firewood and picking up logs.

"DRY" KIT FOR EVENING

- Evenings are slightly cooler in the rainforest, and you may even feel a little chilly at around four or five o'clock in the morning. Average temperatures at night are 20°–25°C (68°–77°F).
- A long-sleeved shirt and pants of slightly heavier material helps protect against bites. Tracksuit bottoms are fine, but avoid jeans, which most people find too heavy and rather uncomfortable.
- Thin fleece.
- Keep on boots in the evening for protection against scorpions and snakes.
- Gumboots for traipsing round in a particularly muddy camp.
- A sarong is a versatile piece of jungle kit. It can be worn when changing or washing, used as a pillow or even as a towel.

HOW DO YOU stay dry in a rainforest?

To live successfully in an extreme environment you will usually need to develop a whole new mentality. In the case of the jungle, forget that quaint idea you've probably cultivated in "civilization" that you need to stay dry most of the time. To enjoy the rainforest experience you must embrace the feeling of being continually soaked to the skin and hot, sweaty, and muddy. It can actually be quite liberating, besides which it is completely unavoidable.

Traveling through the Jungle

Sometimes trekking in a rainforest feels like a stroll in the park, but more often it's an almighty struggle battling against rain and humidity, treacherous slopes, logs and roots, swamps and streams, spiky plants, dense undergrowth, ants, mosquitoes, and leeches—not to mention snakes, scorpions, and a host of other dangerous creatures.

Amid all this you also somehow have to find your way and avoid getting separated from the group. Expert local guides are vital. Not only will they know safe routes, they'll also be aware of the dangers posed by local plants and wildlife and how to avoid them.

SAFE USE OF MACHETES

A machete is designed to be one of the heaviest and sharpest knives in existence. It is a lethal weapon and must be treated with extreme respect:

- Put your machete away in its sheath the moment you finish with it.

DO YOU REALLY need to slash through the undergrowth?

Machetes are an absolutely essential tool in the rainforest, but not primarily for slashing through dense foliage as in the movies. Most of the time you should try to follow paths and trails in the jungle, and if the going gets really tough you're often better off going around the worst of it, rather than using vast amounts of energy to slash straight through (often with no idea if it's going to

thin out). It's also pretty irresponsible to cut down stuff unnecessarily. You may just destroy the sapling of a hardwood tree.

You will, however, use a machete all the time when preparing your camp and sleeping area (see Sleeping in the Jungle, page 108). Machetes are as dangerous as they are indispensable, and must be used incredibly carefully.

- To cut safely put your right foot forward if right-handed (and put your left forward if left-handed). This avoids swinging into your leg. Swing away from your body.
- Watch out for other people: imagine a huge bubble around your body made by the tip of the machete with your arm outstretched, and ensure nobody is within the bubble or nearby.
- Never stick a machete in the ground. Someone may not notice it and slice their foot in two walking by.
- Don't try to cut at the breakneck speed of the local guides. They'll probably have been using a machete since they were infants.

PROBLEM PLANTS

Many vines, plants, and trees have extremely sharp thorns or spikes attached. If you get your backpack or clothes tangled in a thorny vine, moving forwards is impossible. Often known colloquially as "wait-a-while" vines, if you get caught in them you have to backtrack and untangle yourself or, more likely, get a colleague to do it for you.

LOST!

Probably the most common way to get lost is to make a quick pit stop without telling anybody. The expedition walks on, and by the time they realize you're not at the back of the line you're in deep jungle and deep trouble. Strict use of the buddy system should ensure this doesn't happen, as your buddy will be watching out for you (see Safety, page 10).

However, if you do get lost, don't panic. This is where your emergency kit and planning kicks in. The worst thing you can do is run around like a headless chicken. You'll get even more confused and waste valuable energy and water. Instead, stop and think. Reassure yourself that you have water and a little food in your emergency kit, so staying put is not a bad first option.

Rather than you searching for the rest of the expedition, it will probably be far easier for them to retrace their steps and head for where they last saw you. Blow six times on your whistle, and repeat every minute. If that starts to drive you mad, the buttresses of some rainforest trees make great jungle drums.

But if time passes and you want to start trying to rescue yourself, mark your current position clearly so it can't be missed by would-be rescuers. For example, chop down branches and make a cross, and/or hang material from trees and leave a prominent note saying what you are doing.

This is where it's useful to know the general location of a river or a major trail, and whether it might lead you to safety. Use your compass to travel on a set bearing towards it, cutting a clear trail and counting paces. You should be able to retrace your steps back to your start point if it becomes clear you're mistaken. You can then try again in a different direction. As you go, note water sources and good locations for emergency shelters in case you need to spend the night out (see Emergency Survival, page 200).

HOW DO YOU find your way in the jungle?

Jungles are a complete nightmare for finding your way around because you really can't see the wood for the trees! It doesn't matter how good a sense of direction you think you have—one tree looks just like another and you can be completely disorientated in seconds. Even experienced guides and adventurers make mistakes. There are many stories of folk heading a couple of yards away from the group to have a pee, and ending up lost for days.

Handheld GPS (satellite navigation) devices are often not much use, as it's hard to get a signal under the canopy. Where possible, rely on guides or stick to known tracks, otherwise it's time to fall back on old-fashioned navigation methods—using compasses and pacing out distances. Try also to build up a picture of where the main streams, rivers, and trails are, and whether they lead to camps or villages. This could be particularly useful if you become lost.

Drinking Water

Although you'd never want to put it to the test, humans can survive for weeks without food. Water is another matter. Without it you'd last just a few days, and probably less in the heat of a jungle. It's an extraordinary fact that more than half our body weight is made up of water, which is in the blood, the muscles, the brain, and so on. Lose just a few percent of that water and you'll be suffering from dehydration. A loss of ten percent is life-threatening (see Staying Healthy, page 92).

Whatever you're doing in the rainforest, water should never be far from your mind—or lips. As well as keeping drinking, you need to think constantly about where you're going to get your next supply, and how you're going to purify it.

COLLECTING WATER

If in a camp for an extended period of time it may be possible to set up a system for collecting rainwater, but usually you'll be searching for streams or rivers. Always avoid stagnant ponds— the ideal is fast-flowing, clear water low on mud and sand. Point your container downstream to avoid picking up surface debris. (In an emergency situation in the rainforest, there are other sources of water, see page 202.)

PURIFYING WATER

If the water is really cloudy, the sediment will first have to be filtered out. Hi-tech devices are often

HOW DO YOU get clean water to drink?

It's hard enough carrying the weight of water you need for a single day in the jungle (at least 5 kg/ 11 lbs), so bringing in the water you'll need for an entire expedition is simply not an option. Instead you will have to rely on natural sources like streams and rivers, but you should never rely on them to be pure.

Water in the tropics can carry a huge range of diseases and organisms, from cholera, typhoid, and dysentery to things like leeches, which are not fun if they get inside your body. Local people and animals drinking water from a stream or waterhole is no guarantee that it is safe for you. They may have developed a natural resistance to the diseases.

There are various ways to purify water, the most common on expedition being either to boil it or use drops of iodine.

cumbersome and unnecessary. A cloth or simple product called a Millbank bag should do the trick. Note that the water will still need to be purified.

Add a set number of drops of iodine, shake, and leave for half an hour. The exact number of drops is important and will depend on various factors such as temperature, level of contamination, and strength of the iodine solution.

Alternatively, boil the water for a couple of minutes. This should be what's called a full rolling boil with big bubbles.

In a busy expedition camp there needs to be a foolproof system for marking: a) which water is safe to drink, b) which is in the process of being purified, and c) which is still awaiting purification. It can easily get confusing with very serious consequences.

Some find the taste of "iodined" water pretty awful (a bit like getting a mouthful of chlorinated swimming-pool water). Powdered sachets of flavoring can help in making sure enough fluid gets drunk.

EXPEDITION FOOD

It's perhaps ironic that in the rainforest—this diverse, natural larder which has sustained tribespeople for generations—you will still probably be tucking largely into instant expedition food.

The problem is that fresh food rots extremely quickly in the hot, humid environment, and catching jungle animals can be very time-consuming. You need a lot of expertise and local knowledge (see Emergency Survival, page 200).

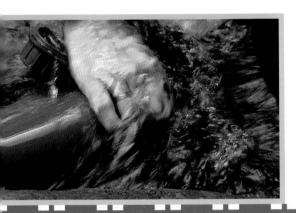

Water bottles should be filled from a fast-flowing stream if possible, pointing the bottle away from the direction of flow to avoid debris being collected.

Iodine drops need to be counted in carefully to ensure the water is fully purified.

Rainforest Camps

A jungle camp can be a very special place, remembered with great nostalgia (the memory tends to blank out the unsavory bits). Turning an inhospitable bit of jungle into a home away from home in just a few hours takes some organizing, whether it's for a long-term base or just the briefest of overnight stops. In either case the camp will need to be safe and hygienic, and when the expedition moves on no lasting environmental damage should be left behind.

SETTING UP CAMP

Nightfall is regular as clockwork in a tropical rainforest: it starts to get pretty gloomy at about five o'clock, the mosquitoes come out with a vengeance, and the sun goes down around six. Less than an hour later the forest is pitch black. You really don't want to be washing or setting up sleeping areas in the dark, so the cut-off to start making camp needs to be about three o'clock in the afternoon. There's a lot to be done, including:

- Choosing a location for the camp. As ever, this is ideally one for expert eyes. Being close to flowing water is a top priority, but you must be sure the site's not going to flood. Trees need to be scoured carefully for possible deadfall, for example, dead branches trapped in vines.
- Configuring the layout: the camp needs areas for sleeping, washing, toilets, communal cooking and eating, and disposing of food waste (slops).
- Setting up sleeping areas (hammocks not tents—see page 108).
- Digging toilets and slops pits.
- Collecting and purifying water.
- Collecting firewood.
- Washing.

The camp layout is determined by hygiene and safety. An expedition of, say, ten or twelve people takes up a surprisingly large area and you won't always be able to find the ideal site. If you are staying for more than a day or two, it gives you a good opportunity to make the camp more homely, perhaps by crafting a table and chairs, screening the toilet trench, making a jungle shower, and so on.

WASHING

While your appearance is going to be far rougher and more "natural" than back home, it's important to wash "bits and pits" (see page 94) and get the sweat off at the end of the day. It's also a chance to wash out your "wet kit." It's often safe to wash in a stream so long as you avoid the period from sunset to dawn. Check if the locals do it and take expert advice.

In their long-term camp, the Serious Jungle team built a small platform over a stream that they used for washing themselves, because they found that wading in the mud to wash was leaving them dirtier than when they started. They used a cup to scoop water over themselves from a larger water container.

EXPEDITION SHOWER

A camp shower can be bought, but it's more stuff to carry through the jungle. Instead it can be improvised by making small holes in the bottom of a bucket or large tin.

Fill the container with water, winch it up over the branch of a tree, and you have a top shower. Heat up the water for added luxury.

?—HOW DO YOU go to the bathroom in the jungle?

This is the world of the "pee tree," "squat spot," and "poo pit." In other words, there should be different areas for pooing and peeing. Doing separate "number ones" and "number twos" can take a little getting used to, but it gives the poo the best chance of breaking down quickly, a process slowed down by urine. The waste is also much less smelly if not mixed together.

For peeing, each sex has separate areas— the "pee tree" and "squat spot" (it's fairly obvious which is that). For pooing, the expedition needs to dig a shallow toilet trench, the "poo pit." The idea is to squat over the trench and afterwards cover the waste with ash from the fire and soil to deodorize it and keep flies off. Each person "goes" a little further along the trench.

Locate the trench a little away from the communal camp area for modesty and to avoid smells, but ensure there is a simple, foolproof route back. Cut a small trail if necessary, or make a rope handrail to guide you. Getting disorientated at night after going to the toilet is all too easy.

Toilet paper will need to be kept in a waterproof bag, and should be burnt rather than buried after use. Remember also to be rigorous about washing hands in antiseptic solution after paying a visit.

The trench should be refilled on breaking camp (one of those "short-straw" jobs). If you are in an area where others are likely to come and camp, mark the refilled trench with crossed branches as a warning.

This simple "poo pit" has been dug for a temporary overnight camp—a long trench will usually be unnecessary for just one night.

FIRES

Making a fire in the jungle is an essential survival skill. It may seem easy but can actually be quite challenging if you don't have exactly the right materials to hand. The principle is to build up the fire in three stages:

- Tinder: wood shavings or any other materials like scrunched up paper or cotton wool balls, which will light quickly and easily. Set tinder alight with matches or a lighter.
- Kindling: in turn use the tinder to light kindling, such as small twigs or bits of bark. To get the kindling to take, you may need to get oxygen in by blowing underneath. Patience is needed at this point to build up the fire slowly and avoid putting it out.
- Fuel: put on larger pieces of wood while leaving an area underneath for air to get in. It is best to use dead wood because live wood is full of sap and hard to burn.

Check whether you have materials that will speed the process along. For instance, soak the kindling in a little paraffin or cooking fuel.

Starting a fire without matches or lighter—for example, by rubbing two sticks together or by creating a spark—is quite a party trick. However, it can be pretty exhausting and should be unnecessary as long as you have good waterproof matches in your emergency kit.

FIRE SAFETY TIPS

Phrases like "playing with fire," "spreading like wildfire," and "getting your fingers burnt" say it all. Fires are potentially hugely dangerous.

- Before leaping in, learn the various skills from an experienced expedition guide or leader.
- Create a "fire-break," a dead area of at least 1 m (3 ft) around the fire, which is clear of anything that could catch fire.
- Watch out for overhanging branches that could ignite as the fire gets bigger.
- Have water, sand, or soil on hand to douse the fire if necessary.
- Beware of flammable materials as you lean over a fire, for example, a sweat rag dangling from your belt.
- Always put out the fire completely. Soak with water and turn logs over to check they're not still red and smoldering underneath.

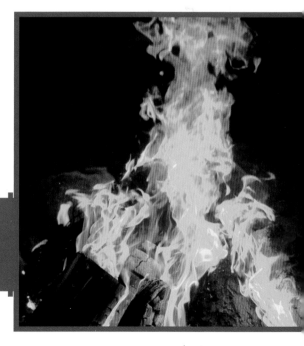

?–HOW DO YOU make a fire when all the wood is wet?

Although this can be done it's not easy, especially when you're cold, wet, and miserable. So if possible it's always worth collecting wood and kindling when the forest is dry, and storing it where it won't get wet. If you forget you'll certainly be kicking yourself in the inevitable downpour, but all is not lost.

Try to find wood that is not soaked right through, which means avoiding wood lying on the ground where possible. For example, look for branches resting in bushes. Use a machete or knife to chop away the wettest outer layers of the wood, leaving thin sticks. If the sticks are already quite thin, make "firesticks" by cutting a series of grooves to expose the drier, inside wood.

If it's still raining you will need a relatively sheltered area to light the fire. You can put up a tarpaulin or basha sheet but will need to take it down for safety as soon as the fire is fully lit. You must ensure you "keep your tinder dry." If you have candles or even a few firelighters thoughtfully packed for just these conditions, now is the moment for you to be deeply smug and produce them.

Putting up the thin sticks in a teepee shape around the tinder and kindling is often very useful, as the small flames help dry them out further so they take.

Now this all sounds fine on paper, but it can be frustrating in the extreme when the fledgling fire goes out at the last minute and you have to start again. Practicing the techniques before the expedition when you're not actually soaked to the skin could be time very well spent.

Sleeping in the Jungle

For some there is nothing more magical than sleeping in the heart of the rainforest, surrounded by a symphony of natural sounds from an extraordinary range of wildlife. Heavy rain, lightning, and thunder add to the spine-tingling sense of being at one with the primeval forces of nature. For others every sound is a spine-chilling threat. Could that rustling be a wild animal about to attack? Are scorpions or spiders crawling into the sleeping bag? It's going to be a very long night.

SETTING UP YOUR HAMMOCK

- Having found a couple of trees the right distance apart, the first thing to do is always to put up the waterproof basha sheet in case it starts raining.
- Then clear the area underneath with your machete to ensure there are no sharp roots, and no scorpions or other bugs lurking.
- Put up the hammock tightly, remembering to slot on the tennis ball halves before tying off the cords (see below).
- Put up the mosquito net.

HOW DO YOU sleep safely among snakes and scorpions?

The answer is reassuring and very simple. You get off the ground and sleep in a hammock slung between two trees. Above the hammock is a waterproof sheet known as a basha. There is also a mosquito net, which tucks in so you are completely cocooned.

Don't worry about snakes and bugs being able to crawl down the cords of the hammock. This is highly unlikely and for added protection the cords can be covered with strong deet (insect repellent). Half a tennis ball stops rain running along the cord and wetting the hammock.

Once you get used to a hammock it's very comfortable, but turning over is a little tricky. Several Serious adventurers literally woke with a bump to find themselves lying on the forest floor.

The hammock can be fully covered by the mosquito net above, and the whole sleeping area is protected by a waterproof basha sheet.

DO YOU NEED a sleeping bag in a tropical rainforest?

Perhaps surprisingly, yes. You'll be acclimated to tropical conditions, and hammocks provide little insulation as the temperature falls as low as 20°C (68°F) just before dawn. While you may go to sleep using the sleeping bag simply to lie on, you'll probably need to pull it over you during the night.

- Lay out your sleeping bag on the hammock, check it for bugs, and tuck the mosquito net in under the bag to create a bug-free area.
- Lay out a roll-mat under the hammock to stand on when you take off your boots.

SPECIALIST JUNGLE HAMMOCKS

As with much specialist kit, there is certainly debate over the best hammock arrangement in the jungle. Some people swear by specialist all-in-one hammocks, which include the waterproof sheet and mosquito net in the design. They are completely enclosed and you usually have to crawl in through a flap underneath the hammock in order to get inside.

Advantages include no wasted time and discomfort as you struggle to ensure the mosquito net is tucked in, no danger of falling out when you turn over, and a greater sense of security as you feel like you're in a cocoon.

Disadvantages include greater expense, possible claustrophobia, and reduced flexibility on a long expedition when you may experience different sleeping arrangements. If the kit is separate, hammocks can, for example, be slung in huts and basha sheets can be used for protection from rain during the day.

Serious

Mountains have always held a special attraction for the human race. Believed to be the homes of the gods in ancient times, they have throughout history provided a spiritual retreat from the stresses of everyday life. With the world stretching out beneath you there is an extraordinary feeling of being at one with nature. While there will always be some who can't understand the appeal of an exhausting climb, the emotions on reaching a summit can be almost indescribable and the views are, of course, awesome.

It's a mistake to think all mountains need specialist climbing skills in order to climb them. Many are effectively no more than a steep trek, but even so they must be treated with great respect and need careful planning.

Andes

THE WORLD'S HIGHEST PEAKS

Adventurers talk of being a 6,000 m or an 8,000 m mountaineer (climbing to 20,000 ft or 26,000 ft), as these represent key achievements in climbing.

The Himalayas in Asia is by far the world's highest mountain range, topped by Everest and containing all 14 of the world's 8,000 m (26,000 ft) peaks (though several of these are in a sub-range called the Karakorams, which some classify as separate to the Himalayas).

The Andes in South America, the world's second highest range, has the distinction of being the world's longest, stretching 7,250 km (4,500 miles) all the way down the west side of South America from Venezuela to Cape Horn.

The world's highest mountains on each continent are known by climbers as the "Seven Summits." Only around one hundred people have climbed them all.

ON TOP OF THE WORLD

More than two thousand climbers have reached the summit of Mount Everest since it was first conquered in 1953 by Sir Edmund Hillary and Sherpa Tenzing Norgay. They include the Serious Andes assistant leader Polly Murray, who became the first Scottish woman to summit Everest in 2000.

Around two hundred have died in the attempt, and many frozen bodies remain on the mountain, a spine-chilling sight for any climber hoping to conquer the world's highest mountain.

IS CLIMBING mountains risky?

Even crossing a road can of course be incredibly risky if not tackled correctly (see Safety, page 10), and the same certainly applies to mountain climbing. As ever, preparation and local knowledge is all-important.

If a mountain involves no rock or ice climbing with ropes, then the right equipment and preparation plus local, experienced guides should ensure anyone of reasonable fitness can attempt it safely. It is, however, worth bearing in mind that even if you make the summit, getting back down is often no picnic for exhausted climbers, actually resulting in more casualties than the ascent.

The risks increase greatly for more difficult, "technical" climbs, especially as mountaineers are always pushing the limits, taking the minimum amount of kit, and attempting ever more challenging routes.

Safety is impossible to guarantee on the handful of mountains over 7,600 m (25,000 ft) that have claimed many lives. Mountaineers talk of entering the "death zone." This is where the lack of oxygen means they can survive for only a very limited time before they need to get back below 7,600 m (25,000 ft). It's also incredibly cold, and the weather can turn in minutes.

On Mount Everest itself, for example, climbers often have a long wait for just the right weather pattern before starting a summit attempt. Even so, the weather can suddenly change so dramatically that they may get stuck near the top in subzero temperatures without hope of rescue.

THE WORLD'S HIGHEST PEAKS

Asia	Everest (Nepal/China border)	8,850 m (29,035 ft
South America	Aconcagua (Argentina)	6,962 m (22,840 ft
North America	Mt. McKinley (Alaska, USA)	6,195 m (20,320 ft
Africa	Kilimanjaro (Tanzania)	5,895 m (19,340 ft
Europe	Elbrus (Russia)	5,633 m (18,481 ft
Antarctica	Vinson Massif	4,897 m (16,067 ft
Australia/Oceania	Carstensz Pyramid (Indonesia)	4,884 m (16,023 ft

The Serious Andes team's greatest challenge was to climb the volcano Cotopaxi, which soars to almost 6,000 m (20,000 ft).

The Serious Andes Adventure

The Serious Andes expedition took place close to the equator, but was far from a typical tropical experience. The team flew into the South American country of Ecuador (the name means equator in Spanish), and as they landed in the capital Quito they were already at an altitude higher than most ski resorts.

At 2,800 m (9,300 ft) Quito is the second-highest capital in the world after La Paz in Bolivia, and as a result it's much cooler than most cities in the tropics. Some travelers have breathing problems and need oxygen before they've even left the airport. The adventurers were surprised at how they became breathless just walking up a flight of stairs to their hotel room.

Before heading up into the Andes, the team got a chance to visit the endangered animals they would be helping—two beautiful, spectacled bears called Leo and Beto. They were living at a rescue center in a tiny cage. The Serious Andes mission was to build a much larger, semi-wild enclosure at 3,750 m (12,500 ft) to help return them to the wild (see page 121).

The enclosure would be built in a private reserve called Yanahurco, a four-hour drive on dirt tracks into the mountains. On arrival the adventurers immediately suffered the effects of the thin mountain air—wheezing and gasping on a ten minute hike to their camp. They experienced

The young adventurers headed up into the Andes by bus, traveling on dirt tracks through the spectacular Cotopaxi National Park.

other typical effects of altitude, including nausea, mild headaches, and difficulty sleeping, but thankfully nobody developed more serious altitude sickness.

The expedition doctors examined the team every day as part of the first-ever study of how twelve- to fifteen-year-olds cope at high altitude (see page 130). On the first evening in camp they found characteristic changes taking place, as their bodies fought to cope with the lack of oxygen in the air. Breathing was much faster and blood pressure was up, but even so oxygen levels in the blood were still about 10 percent lower than normal, making almost any activity exhausting. While it is nothing unusual on first reaching

altitude, an oxygen level this low at sea level would count as a medical emergency.

The huge enclosure included a perimeter fence of 100 m (330 ft), all of which would have to be concreted into the ground to prevent the bears escaping. Working at altitude in the cold and rain put great strain on the group, leading to bickering and arguments. Several of the adventurers came close to throwing in the towel, but in the end the difficulties made completing the enclosure all the more rewarding. Working in appalling weather, they took just a week to build the entire bear-proof structure at altitude on the side of a hill, an extraordinary achievement for eight young adventurers.

The Serious Andes enclosure during construction in its natural setting on the side of a hill at 3,750 m (12,500 ft).

The Serious Andes enclosure was officially opened by the British Ambassador and Ecuador's Tourism Minister, who hailed the team as "an example to other children all round the world." Spectacled bears Leo and Beto took to the enclosure immediately, and after a week of rehabilitation they were at last released to the wild, a sight the adventurers would never forget.

But the expedition was far from over. The challenge they'd been building up was now quite literally looming large. They were going to try to go higher than any team their age by climbing the volcano Cotopaxi. At almost 6,000 m (20,000 ft), the leaders did not expect more than three or four at best to make it to the top, and they thought it most unlikely that the two smallest members of the team, twelve-year-old Josh and thirteen-year-old Caitlin, would get very far. This was purely a function of their size—the smaller and thinner you are the more easily you get cold, and the less your reserves of energy and strength.

The attempt would be made in three stages, with a night spent at advance base camp (4,800 m/ 16,000 ft) and another at camp one (5,100 m/ 17,000 ft) before a huge final push for the summit. The enormity of what they'd taken on hit home during the very first leg of the ascent. It looked easy enough—just 300 m (1,000 ft), and they hadn't even hit the snowline yet. But walking on loose volcanic gravel was utterly exhausting, and at nearly 5 km (3 miles) above sea level there was only half as much oxygen in the air. Several adventurers suffered panic attacks, feeling they couldn't breathe, and one of the girls had to descend because she was suffering with the first symptoms of altitude sickness.

The rest all made it through to advance base camp, and were now higher than Mont Blanc, the highest mountain in Western Europe. But it wasn't long before a second adventurer got altitude sickness, and another dream of making the summit was over.

From advance base camp onwards, almost all the climb was on snow and ice. The extreme effort

The spectacled bears wore radio collars so they could be tracked after their return to the wild.

of climbing a steep glacier led to more panic attacks, but with a superhuman effort all six remaining adventurers made it to camp one. And to the surprise of the leaders, that included both Josh and Caitlin.

Their reward was one of the most stunning camp sites on earth, though the combination of high altitude, strong winds, uneven ground, and a three AM wake-up call meant sleeping was all but impossible for the team.

During the night the temperature fell to −10°C (14°F), and it was a tired and very cold group of young adventurers who set off in the dark at four AM on the final leg of their record attempt. To reach the summit they faced a marathon round trip of at least ten hours up fifty degree slopes, a challenge that would defeat many adult adventurers.

Within minutes of setting off there was a major blow. One of the older boys was suffering from an upset stomach and didn't have the strength to carry on. Now there were five, and they were having a rough time of it, inching slowly upwards through the darkness with agonizingly cold feet.

Seeing dawn break from so high up the mountain was awe-inspiring, but before long Josh started to have trouble breathing. Having reached 5,300 m (17,500 ft) he could go no further, and although hugely disappointed it was an incredible effort for a twelve-year-old to get so high.

It left just four adventurers with a chance of getting to the top, though they were still half a mile below the summit. Defying all predictions thirteen-year-old Caitlin was still hanging in, 88 lbs of sheer determination. If they could avoid altitude sickness and sheer exhaustion it was now all "in the head." How strong was their willpower, and how much did they really want to make it to the top?

They battled onwards and upwards for six-and-a-half gruelling hours, and remarkably Caitlin, Erin, Kylie, and Will all made it to the summit, the youngest group on record ever to go so high.

First sight of the daunting climb up Cotopaxi from base camp at 4,500 m (15,000 ft).

EXPEDITION LOCATION

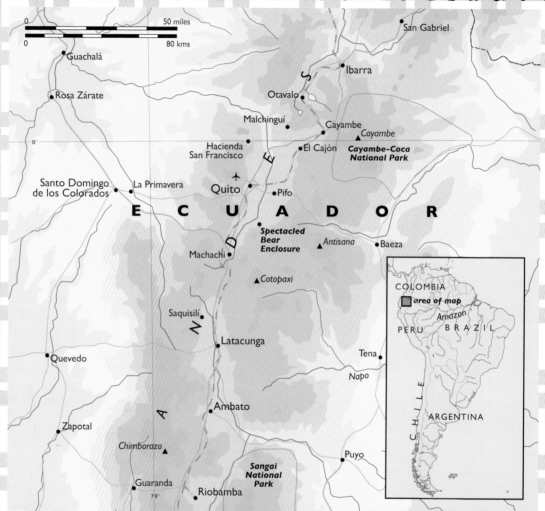

0 | 50 miles
0 | 80 kms

San Gabriel

Guachalá

Rosa Zárate

Ibarra

Otavalo

Malchinguí

Cayambe
Cayambe

Hacienda
San Francisco

El Cajón

**Cayambe-Coca
National Park**

Santo Domingo
de los Colorados

La Primavera

Quito

Pifo

E C U A D O R

**Spectacled
Bear
Enclosure**

Machachi

Antisana

Baeza

Cotopaxi

Saquisilí

Latacunga

Quevedo

Tena

Napo

Ambato

Zapotal

Chimborazo

Puyo

**Sangai
National
Park**

Guaranda

Riobamba

COLOMBIA

area of map

Amazon

PERU | BRAZIL

CHILE

ARGENTINA

The Serious Andes base camp lay 4,500 m
(15,000 ft) up on the slopes of Cotopaxi,
Ecuador's second hightest mountain.

COTOPAXI

"When I was but thirteen or so
I went into a golden land.
Chimborazo, Cotopaxi
Took me by the hand."

(From *"Romance"* by W. J. Turner)

Set in the heart of Ecuador's "Avenue of the Volcanoes," Cotopaxi (5,897 m/19,346 ft) is Ecuador's second-highest mountain after Chimborazo. Its perfect, snow-capped volcanic cone is almost half a mile across, and is the stuff of legend and poetry. It is one of the highest active volcanoes in the world, though its last major eruption was more than one hundred years ago.

While it needs no "technical" rock-climbing, its glaciers are full of dangerous crevasses. It is essential to have the right kit and experienced local guides.

Many tackle the summit from a climbing hut at 4,800 m (16,000 ft), setting off soon after midnight, but the Serious Andes leadership team added in an extra camp at 5,100 m (17,000 ft). This was not an immediate decision. The benefits of breaking the journey had to be weighed against the debilitating effects of a poor night's sleep at such high altitude.

The four young adventurers celebrate their record-breaking climb with the leadership team and expert local guides.

Andean Wildlife

The Andes is home to some very distinctive animals found nowhere else in the world. The four South American members of the camel family—the llama, alpaca, guanaco, and vicuña—have become a symbol of the continent. Two flagship species, the spectacled bear and the Andean condor, are highly endangered. Little wildlife is found above about 4,000 m (13,000 ft).

SPECTACLED BEAR

The only bear found in South America, spectacled bears take their name from the distinctive white markings around the eyes. Known also as Andean bears, they roam from cloud forests on the lower slopes of the Andes to higher Andean grasslands (known as the Paramo) above the treeline. They are one of the smallest of all bears, with the adult male weighing around 160 kg (350 lbs), double an average man.

Spectacled bears are great climbers, making platforms in trees to rest on by pulling down branches, and they're also able to climb steep rock faces. They are largely vegetarian, but will occasionally eat small mammals.

THREATS TO SPECTACLED BEARS

The rare bear is teetering on the brink of extinction, with only a few thousand thought to be left in the wild.

The main threat is destruction of its habitat. Cloud forests are being logged and cut down for grazing at an alarming rate, and the Paramo is also being turned into farmland.

As their traditional foods disappear, the bears have developed a taste for crops like sweetcorn (and have even been known to attack cattle), so farmers will often shoot them. Cubs may be illegally sold as pets or to perform in circuses, and are often kept in appalling conditions.

Some captive bears have been confiscated by police and taken to rescue centers. It is hoped that eventually many of these will be returned to the wild, which is where the Serious Andes team played their part.

THE ANDEAN BEAR CONSERVATION PROJECT

Rehabilitating any animal is difficult and risky, especially if it's been in captivity for most of its life. It may no longer have the skills to find food, and it may be too trusting of humans who could see it as a threat—or a valuable prize.

Serious Andes worked with an Ecuadorian charity, the Andean Bear Conservation Project, to build a large semi-wild enclosure at altitude. The enclosure was a crucial element in the final stage of rehabilitating the captive bears.

The 700 sq m (7,500 sq ft) Serious Andes enclosure is located on the side of a hill in the territory of the bear's natural home. The bears are brought here from rescue centers, allowing them to get used to the altitude and learn to live in the terrain they'll encounter in the wild. The charity's researchers gradually encourage them to forage for their own food, judging when they are ready for release into the surrounding private Yanahurco reserve—an almost uninhabited, protected area where the bears can hopefully thrive without human interference.

ANDEAN CONDOR

The endangered Andean condor is the world's largest bird of prey, with a wingspan of more than 3 m (10 ft)—about the same as the length of a small car. The huge bird is absolutely majestic in flight, soaring effortlessly on the wind, but many find this bald-headed member of the vulture family less attractive close up.

Andean condors have been reported soaring at altitudes above 6,000 m (20,000 ft). They mate for life, roosting and laying eggs on ledges in rock faces above 3,000 m (10,000 ft), producing only

An anaesthetised spectacled bear is returned to the wild by the Serious Andes team (left).

one chick every two years. The chick takes around six months to fly and is dependent on its parents for a further two years.

This slow, intensive reproduction pattern means the Andean condor population can all too easily suffer a dramatic fall in size. Their main threat is humans, who shoot the bird illegally for sport - or in the mistaken belief that it will take their farm animals. In fact, condors are scavengers, feeding almost exclusively on the remains of dead animals. There are thought to be just a few thousand left, though numbers are hard to estimate because the birds are found only in very remote areas.

LLAMA

Along with the alpaca, vicuña, and guanaco, these South American relatives of the camel have no humps, and are well adapted to life at altitude.

To cope with the lack of oxygen in the air, their blood has evolved to extract oxygen from the air more efficiently, as well as having more red blood cells to carry it round the body. All have thick woollen coats to protect them from the cold.

Llamas and alpacas have been kept as domesticated farm animals for thousands of years. Alpaca wool is particularly prized for its softness, while coarser llama wool is used to make things like ropes and saddle-bags.

-ARE SPECTACLED BEARS dangerous?

Spectacled bears were the inspiration for the children's story of Paddington Bear (who of course came from Peru). But, much as you may want to stroke or cuddle one, they are extremely powerful with strong, sharp claws and should never be approached.

Having said that, they are not aggressive by nature and there are no cases on record of a spectacled bear attacking a human except in self-defense. They are in fact very hard to spot in the wild as they will flee at the sight—or smell— of a human.

Llamas have traditionally served many other purposes as well. They provide milk and meat, their dung is used for fuel, and their fat for candles. Like their camel cousins, they are also beasts of burden, and have the ability to carry large loads over long distances.

CHINCHILLA

This small rodent, pictured below, is around 25 cm (10 in) long, excluding the tail, and has the densest—and many believe the softest—fur of any animal. While humans have just one hair growing out of each follicle, a chinchilla usually has more than fifty incredibly fine hairs per follicle.

Found only in the Andes, it is highly endangered, having been hunted almost to extinction for its beautiful fur. Though now protected, captive animals are still bred for the fur trade.

Into Thin Air

Human survival depends on breathing oxygen, but the higher you go the thinner the air gets and the more the body struggles to cope. Most healthy people who live around sea level first start to notice the effects above 2,500 m (8,000 ft), usually defined as the start of high altitude.

Your breathing and heart rates increase to compensate for the lower oxygen levels, and gentle activity may leave you much more breathless than you'd expect. This is normal and after a few days your body should acclimatize.

If, however, you get a range of other persistent symptoms including headache and nausea, you may be suffering the first stages of altitude sickness. You should go no higher, and may also need to descend to lower altitude for a while.

OXYGEN LEVELS

We live at the bottom of an "ocean" of air. This gets ever thinner as you travel away from the earth's surface, till there is almost no air around 80 km (50 miles) up on the borders of space. At

SERIOUS ANDES ALTITUDE CHART

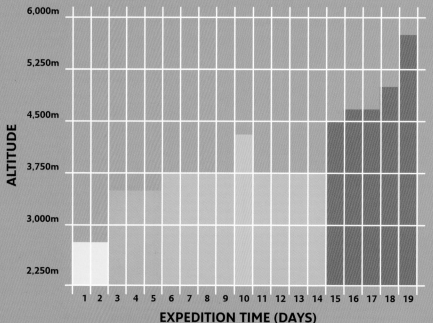

Chart showing how the expedition was planned, giving team members time to acclimatize before moving on to a higher altitude.

Key
- Acclimatization Quito
- Mountain training
- Bear enclosure
- Altitude training trek
- Cotopaxi ascent

ALTITUDE

6,000m
5,250m
4,500m
3,750m
3,000m
2,250m

1 2 3 4 5 6 7 8 9 10 11 12 13 14 15 16 17 18 19

EXPEDITION TIME (DAYS)

3,000 m (10,000 ft) up there is only two-thirds as much oxygen, and by the time you reach 4,500 m (15,000 ft) oxygen levels are down to almost a half.

Anyone hoping to conquer Everest, 8,849 m (29,035 ft) up, will have to cope with about one third of the oxygen found at sea level. This is in fact at the extreme limits of what the human body can cope with, so almost all climbers take extra oxygen to breathe.

ACCLIMATIZATION

Going to high altitude has to be done very gradually to allow the body time to adjust to the lower levels of oxygen, otherwise there is a greater chance of developing altitude sickness. As there is less oxygen in each breath, the body acclimatizes by adapting to take in as much as possible and get it round the body more efficiently. Along with faster, deeper breathing and a higher heart rate, other more gradual changes include an increase in the number of oxygen-transporting red blood cells.

Once you get to about 3,000 m (10,000 ft) you should plan to sleep for a day or two at that altitude before going higher, and then ideally sleep no more than about 300 m (1,000 ft) or so higher each night. The climber's golden rule is "climb high, sleep low," so even if you go much higher during the day you should try to descend to camp only 300 m (1,000 ft) higher than the night before. This strategy will not necessarily prevent altitude sickness, but it will lower the risks. It's worth pointing out that no matter how well acclimatized, a climber's body will not perform as well at high altitude as at sea-level.

The Serious Andes expedition was carefully planned to help acclimatization, with a gradual overall increase in altitude (see chart left). A brief training climb on day 10 also helped prepare for higher altitude.

The logistics of the trip meant there were unavoidable large increases in altitude on day 3 and day 15, and the leadership team knew there was a higher risk that someone would need to be taken back down to lower altitude on those days.

ALTITUDE SICKNESS

Also known as acute mountain sickness (AMS), altitude sickness is very common, affecting roughly half of all climbers and tourists at high altitude (though it's worth bearing in mind that many of these won't have spent time acclimatizing fully). Altitude sickness can be fatal if untreated, but at its early stages simply descending 300 m (1,000 ft) or so should lead to a complete recovery within a few hours.

Typical symptoms include a persistent headache, nausea, tiredness, dizziness, and difficulty sleeping, but there is no simple diagnosis to tell you when "feeling a bit rough" in the thin mountain air begins to turn into altitude sickness. This is a serious issue for mountaineers who may be tempted to do the worst thing possible, which is to disregard the signs and press on—with possibly fatal consequences.

-?-WHY DON'T YOU suffer the effects of altitude on a plane?

Modern aircraft are pressurized, which means that as you go higher you are blissfully unaware of the air getting thinner and thinner outside. However, if there's a sudden problem like a window breaking, the cabin will depressurize—with air rushing out until the cabin is at the same low pressure as the outside. It's as if you were suddenly outside at the altitude of the plane, perhaps say 9,000 m (30,000 ft) where there is only around one-third as much oxygen in the air. And because passengers are, of course, completely unacclimatized they'd be unconscious in as little as thirty seconds. Fortunately, "in the unlikely event of sudden cabin depressurisation, oxygen masks will fall from the overhead compartment," and pilots are also trained to descend rapidly to about 3,000 m (10,000 ft).

You may wonder why your ears often pop soon after take-off or as you come in to land. The answer is that airlines actually reduce the cabin pressure a little as the plane climbs after take-off and increase it again as the plane comes in to land.

It's not a dramatic reduction—typically similar to being at 1,500-2,500 m (5,000-8,000 ft). But if the change from sea level air pressure isn't done gradually enough it can cause some ear pain.

This small reduction in cabin pressure lessens the stress on the cabin walls at very high altitude and means they don't have to be built quite as strong, which would add significantly to the weight of the aircraft.

The Serious Andes adventurers climb way above the clouds on their final push for the summit of Cotopaxi

Altitude specialists have devised a chart (the "Lake Louise AMS score") to help the self-diagnosis of altitude sickness. Below is the version used by Serious Andes.

If possible, use this guide in conjunction with advice from a medic or experienced local guide. The most important thing if you have altitude sickness (AMS) is to GO NO HIGHER. If symptoms persist or get worse you should go down at least 300 m (1,000 ft). You may then feel up to rejoining the expedition within two or three days, and the extra acclimatization means you'll have a reasonable chance of symptoms not recurring.

If the first signs of altitude sickness are ignored and you do carry on climbing, perhaps through a misguided sense of not letting down colleagues or to "prove" you can battle on through pain, then it can quickly turn very serious and may lead to a build-up of fluid in the brain or lungs. Known as HACE (High Altitude Cerebral Edema) and HAPE (High Altitude Pulmonary Edema), both conditions are life-threatening. You will need to descend immediately for treatment. Remember, too, that HAPE can also develop without previous symptoms of AMS.

HIGH ALTITUDE DRUGS

Acetazolamide (trade name Diamox) has been hailed by some as an acclimatization wonder drug, and branded highly dangerous by others. It is in

LAKE LOUISE ALTITUDE SICKNESS (AMS) SCORE

	HEADACHE	GASTRO-INTESTINAL SYMPTOMS	FATIGUE/ WEAKNESS	DIZZINESS/ LIGHT-HEADEDNESS	DIFFICULTY SLEEPING
0	No headache	No gastro-intestinal symptoms	Not tired or weak	Not dizzy	Slept as well as usual
1	Mild headache	Poor appetite or nausea	Mild fatigue/ weakness	Mild dizziness	Did not sleep as well as usual
2	Moderate headache	Moderate nausea or vomiting	Moderate fatigue/ weakness	Moderate dizziness	Woke many times, poor night's sleep
3	Severe headache, incapacitating	Severe nausea & vomiting, incapacitating	Severe fatigue/ weakness, incapacitating	Severe dizziness, incapacitating	Could not sleep at all
Score:					
Total:					

Total score of 3 or more + recent rise in altitude + headache + one other symptom = AMS

fact neither, and the general medical opinion is that if used correctly it can be a valuable extra tool for dealing with altitude sickness.

If you are suffering the effects of AMS, it may help to relieve symptoms. It's important, however, to keep to the golden rule of going no higher, and descending if you continue to feel ill.

Some people also recommend acetazolamide as a preventative measure to take in advance of going to altitude if you know you won't have time to acclimate fully. There is a myth that this will mask AMS symptoms and is therefore dangerous. This isn't the case, though there are side effects such as tingling in lips and fingers, which some find quite unpleasant.

PORTABLE ALTITUDE CHAMBERS

If you develop serious altitude sickness, you'll probably be incapable of getting yourself back down the mountain, and a lightweight portable altitude chamber (or Gamow bag) could be a lifesaver. The bag can be inflated to a much greater pressure than the surrounding air, as if the casualty has instantly been transported to a lower altitude. You need to be inside for several hours, and it can be quite claustrophobic, but afterwards you may be well enough to descend the mountain on your own two feet, avoiding the need for stretchering down (which may be extremely difficult and time-consuming).

DO EXPERIENCED MOUNTAINEERS get altitude sickness?

Ironically, fit young mountaineers are the most likely of all to get altitude sickness. This is because they tend to race up mountains way too fast, and often try to show how "macho" they are by ignoring all aches and pains.

But assuming they act rather more sensibly, the real question is whether experienced high-altitude climbers who've never had altitude sickness might get it in the future. Perhaps surprisingly, the answer is yes. Altitude sickness is brought on by a set of circumstances that aren't fully understood, and mountaineers who have gone for years without a problem may suddenly succumb.

However, what seasoned climbers have proved is that their bodies are generally capable of coping with altitude, and it does seem there is another group of people whose bodies always struggle to go above a certain height. It is impossible to predict if you will fall into this category (it makes no difference how old or athletic you are), but if so you will probably get altitude sickness every time you go up high, and may never get to conquer the highest peaks.

IS IT SAFE to take children to high altitude?

Many mountain guides will tell you that taking children up high holds extra risks of altitude sickness, but their experience may be based on the fact that children tend to get bored easily and run around a lot, exactly the sort of behavior that leads to problems at altitude. There is very little reliable research into young people at high altitude, which is why the Serious Andes team undertook its survey (see page 131). The results suggested that strictly supervised kids aged 12 to 15 actually fare little differently to adults.

Doctors have greater concerns about much younger children, who may not be capable of describing any symptoms of altitude sickness accurately. Being smaller they also lose heat more quickly, increasing the risk of frostbite and hypothermia. But with careful planning many parents have had extremely rewarding treks at altitude with young children.

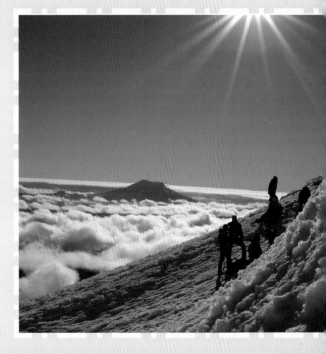

Bottles of oxygen are also a good safety precaution on climbs to altitude, though they should be saved for real emergencies. Mountaineers only tend to start using oxygen for actual climbing above about 7,000 m (23,000 ft).

BLOOD DISORDERS

Coping with the lack of oxygen is a remarkable feat by the body, and there are some blood disorders and conditions that make traveling to altitude extremely dangerous. For example, anyone with sickle cell anemia or thalassaemia is generally advised not to go above 1,500 m (5,000 ft).

Without even knowing it, some completely healthy people have what's called sickle cell trait, which means they carry a sickle cell gene, and this is unfortunately also a serious problem at altitude. If you are of African, Asian, or Mediterranean background, sickle cell is more common, and it's well worth having a simple blood test as a precaution before going to altitude. (The only consolation if you do have sickle cell trait or sickle cell anaemia is that they protect against the worst type of malaria. So, for you it may be a case of diverting from the highest mountains to the deepest jungles).

THE SERIOUS ANDES HIGH ALTITUDE SURVEY

The Serious Andes expedition doctors conducted a major survey of the eight young adventurers (aged twelve to fifteen) as they attempted to climb to a record height of almost 6,000 m (20,000 ft). Each day they took readings of heart and breathing rates, blood pressure, and oxygen concentrations in the blood. The adventurers also filled out Lake Louise altitude sickness scorecards daily.

The thirteen adults on the expedition were monitored for comparison. They ranged from elite 8,000 m (26,000 ft) mountaineers (the expedition leaders) to members of the production team who had never been to high altitude before.

The conclusion was that there was no significant difference between how the adults and the young people coped with the altitude.

The Serious Andes altitude specialist Dr. Stephan Sanders with the portable device used to measure oxygen levels in the blood.

FACTS RELATING TO ALTITUDE STUDY

The survey clearly demonstrated the effects of acclimatization (similar in both the adults and young people):

- Oxygen levels in the blood averaged 90 percent soon after arriving at their training camp at just under 3,750 m (12,500 ft). The normal range at sea level is 95-100 percent.
- After a week, levels had climbed back to an average of 94 percent. This reflects the acclimatization process in which a faster rate of breathing increases oxygen levels.
- On the push for the summit, levels dropped significantly as was expected—averaging 85 percent at camp 1 at 5,100 m (17,000 ft) and 77 percent at 5,700 m (19,000 ft) just below the summit.

Blood oxygen levels for Serious Andes expedition

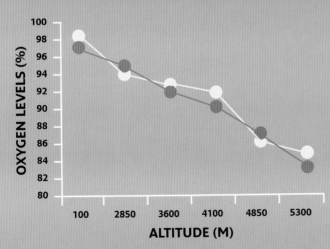

This graph compares blood oxygen levels in kids and adults at varying heights.

○ Kids
● Adults

Extreme Mountain Weather

Mountains couldn't have been better designed to test humans to the limit. As if the lack of oxygen weren't enough, you often have to contend with Arctic conditions, which means frostbite and hypothermia are a constant concern. If the sun does come out it is extremely dangerous, as there is less atmosphere to absorb the harmful UV rays. Then there are deadly avalanches, disorientating white-outs in snowstorms, and thick clouds, plus the small matter of being struck by lightning (a greater risk up high). And that's all before you even think about the extreme dangers of actually climbing.

WHY IS IT always cold at the top of a mountain— isn't it nearer the sun?

Well, yes, but given that the sun is about ninety million miles away, one or two miles is not going to make a whole lot of difference. Other factors are much more important:

- Every 300 m (1,000 ft) you go up, the temperature generally falls by around 2°C (36°F). This is because the rays of the sun hardly heat the air as they go through it, warming the surface of the Earth instead. In turn, the ground heats the air immediately above it, but as a poor conductor of heat the air gets colder the further away it is.
- While hot air certainly rises, it expands and cools as it does so (unless trapped, for example, by your ceiling).

So while it's true that the sun hitting your body will feel just as warm at altitude as at sea level (witness skiers in T-shirts), the air temperature will be much lower. This is a tricky combination for controlling sweating, with hypothermia a real risk as the sun disappears or you climb into a shady area (see Hypothermia, page 30).

This fall in temperature with altitude means that even mountains on the equator like Mount Kilimanjaro in Tanzania and Cotopaxi in Ecuador are covered in snow and ice on their upper slopes.

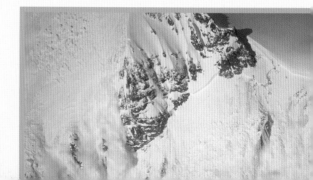

WHAT DO YOU DO if caught in an avalanche?

This is not good news. There are no guarantees you'll survive, so the best plan is to do everything possible to make sure you don't get caught in one in the first place, taking advice from experienced local experts.

If going into avalanche-prone areas always wear an avalanche transceiver (also known as a beacon). This transmits a signal to rescuers in case you get buried. All transceivers use the same frequency and can be switched to receive mode so you can help in a search if necessary.

If you see an avalanche start above you it may be possible to get to the side or take shelter under a rock or tree, though bear in mind that the avalanche could be powerful enough to sweep along everything in its way.

Some avalanches travel quite slowly, and the Serious Adventure leader Polly Murray, an international skier, once managed to ski ahead of an avalanche till she could veer off out of its path.

If caught up in an avalanche don't fight it but go with the flow, concentrating only on staying as near to the surface of the snow as possible. This could be the difference between life and death when the avalanche finally slows to a halt.

Some suggest using swimming strokes as if trying to swim along with a large wave. If possible, dump all kit like skis, poles, and backpack as they will just drag you down and may also injure you.

As the avalanche slows, cover your mouth and nose with your hands to avoid them filling with snow, and if buried try to make as large a breathing area as possible with your arms before the snow packs too tightly around you.

If you are near the surface when you finally come to a halt try to dig yourself out, and if you hear people near you call out, but otherwise stay calm and don't waste what little air you have. Like most advice about not panicking in life-threatening situations this is easier said than done.

Realistically you will have no more than half an hour of air, possibly far less, so the most likely rescue will come not from a search and rescue team but from colleagues who hopefully tracked you when you were being swept down and saw where you disappeared under the snow. Expedition emergency kits—lightweight aluminum shovels and foldaway probes for searching in the snow—will now be worth their weight in gold.

There are the inevitable, heartwarming stories of people being dug out alive after being buried in an avalanche for hours, but the best chance of survival is in the first fifteen minutes so rescuers need to work smart and fast.

MOUNTAIN WINDS

Mountains are notorious for strong winds, a result of being such a large object "in the way" of the weather causing air to be forced over them. Also, mountain ranges act like funnels with the air whistling through mountain passes and valleys at great speed.

Even when it is calm lower down, there will often be a gale blowing near the summit. As well as the cooling effects of wind chill (see page 30), strong winds add greatly to the danger of losing your footing on tricky sections of a climb and every year there are reports of hikers and climbers being literally blown off mountains.

WORLD'S STRONGEST WIND

The fastest surface wind speed ever recorded was on Mount Washington in America. In spring 1934 the observatory at the summit (1,927 m/6,288 ft) measured a gust of 372 km/h (231 mph).

Cold winds tumbling down Antarctic mountains have been known to reach speeds of 320 km/h (200 mph), similar to the strongest winds found inside a hurricane.

PREDICTING AVALANCHES

Avalanches are great masses of snow that race down hillsides and mountains. They are one of the worst nightmares of most mountaineers and

The team wore sunglasses to protect their eyes from the harmful rays of the sun.

skiers, as they are hard to predict and often fatal.

Traveling at up to 240 km/h (150 mph), avalanches may contain thousands of tons of snow and destroy everything in their path. There are two main types of avalanche. Either a huge slab of snow detaches itself and begins to slide down, or a relatively small amount of snow starts tumbling down a slope, gradually building in size as it goes.

There is no substitute for local knowledge of snow conditions and likely avalanche locations. In general, avalanches are more likely after a heavy snowfall, on slopes that bow out (meaning they are convex rather than concave), and on slopes warmed by the sun. The risk increases as the day goes on and snow starts to melt.

Avalanches may be triggered by movement and noise, and most people caught in an avalanche have started it off themselves.

SUNBURN AND SNOWBLINDNESS

Among all your other concerns it's hard to realize that sunburn is a serious threat in the freezing conditions. But with far less atmosphere for the sun's UV rays to travel through you can be sunburnt in minutes. It's absolutely essential to use good sunscreen on any exposed flesh, including, of course, the tops of the ears if not covered by a hat. Similarly, good wrap-around sunglasses must be worn to protect your eyes from snowblindness (see page 29).

The perfect volcanic cone of Cotopaxi looks deceptively tranquil from a distance.

Climbing Mountains

There is all the difference in the world between a hike in the hills and the ascent of one of the planet's great peaks, which may well involve specialist techniques and rock-climbing. What they have in common is that both are potentially hugely dangerous and regularly claim the lives of those attempting to ascend.

Many hikers—and indeed much more experienced climbers—have gotten into serious trouble walking in beautiful areas with low eleveations. In areas under 1,500 m (5,000 ft), the weather can turn just as quickly as on higher peaks, and ill-prepared climbers can all too easily lose their way and freeze to death in near-Arctic conditions.

Proper planning, once again, is the key to safety and success when climbing a mountain. That means having the right gear, checking local conditions and weather forecasts, and when going to high altitude hiring an experienced (English-speaking) local guide.

SAFETY KIT

As well as the usual safety kit (see Safety, page 10), an expedition heading to high altitude should consider carrying a portable altitude chamber and oxygen cylinders. Satellite phones should also be supplemented by walkie-talkies for local communication in case the group gets spread out on the mountain.

If there is the possibility of avalanches, the expedition may also need personal avalanche transceivers, lightweight shovels, and avalanche probes. These are extendable sticks for prodding in the snow to search for victims.

ROCK AND ICE CLIMBING TECHNIQUES

As soon as slopes get too steep to walk or scramble up, ropes become necessary and training will be needed to operate safely.

Among the obstacles you may encounter on a mountain are steep rock faces and ice walls. The basic principle is to be roped up so you can't fall too far. For instance, this is how two climbers might tackle a rock face:

- The lead climber has a rope attached to his harness and sets off up the rock face, looking for hand and foot holds.
- Before going too high he inserts a peg into the rock face. The peg is usually designed to wedge tightly into a crack, avoiding the need to hammer anything in. He clips in his rope using connectors called carabiners.
- The climber on the ground has the other end of the rope tied to an anchor, using a special friction device in his harness to take up slack and support the lead climber in case he falls (this is known as belaying).

WHY DO mountain climbers often set off in the night?

The real reason is that at very high altitudes the climb will inevitably be up snow and ice, and as the day wears on the conditions will usually become more and more treacherous. If the sun hits the mountain the snow may start to melt, and depending on the local conditions there will probably be a much-increased risk of avalanches.

So the aim is to get to the summit—and back down—with time to spare before the risk gets too great. Local guides with experience of the mountain will advise on the cut-off point.

There is also another benefit. Grim as it may be to drag yourself out of your sleeping bag in the freezing cold in the middle of the night, it's certainly much easier to keep at a constant temperature when you get climbing. Once the sun comes up, it's a constant juggle to stop overheating—and cooling down too much in the shade.

MOUNTAIN CLOTHING AND KIT

Temperatures on a mountain may vary wildly in and out of the sun and wind, so making use of the layering system is essential to ensure you don't overheat or get too cold (see Arctic Clothing, page 34). To accommodate the needs of climbing there are some key differences to standard Arctic gear:

- Waterproof jacket extends only to waist to accommodate harness.
- Harness (for rock-climbing or for roping on glaciers and other dangerous areas—not necessary for hiking at lower altitude).
- Ice axe.
- Some prefer fleece leggings to hiking pants for ease of movement when climbing (waterproof overtrousers will still be needed for wet conditions).
- Gaiters keep socks and boots dry when climbing in snow.
- Climbing boots have a rigid sole and grooves to enable crampons to be clipped on.
- Crampons have twelve razor-sharp points and attach to boots for climbing on ice and glaciers (see page 140).
- Helmet.
- Head lamp for climbing in the dark.

- The lead climber continues upwards, inserting more pegs as he goes.
- On reaching the top he anchors his rope and belays the second climber, who takes out the pegs as he ascends.

PANIC ATTACKS

Many trekkers and climbers have had the scary experience of a panic attack at high altitude, suddenly feeling unable to catch their breath. The plus side is that having suffered an attack they probably never will again, as it's easily avoidable.

Panic attacks are a result of overdoing it, usually by walking too fast up a slope, especially if carrying a heavy load. Your body starts gasping for breath as if you've just taken part in an Olympic sprint, but finds there isn't enough oxygen in the air. It's an awful feeling, like a fish out of water, but it usually subsides in under a minute.

The golden rule is to take everything much more slowly than at sea level. Climbing up a hill is all about getting into a regular rhythm without stopping and starting all the time, and a useful mental image is to think of heading up steadily in slow motion.

HIGH FLYER

In 2005 a French Eurocopter helicopter claimed to have touched down briefly on the summit of Everest. While some say it actually landed on a lower peak, the high altitude helicopter has reached similar heights in tests and may pave the way for helicopter rescues at extreme high altitude in the future.

Slow progress heading up a glacier on Cotopaxi. Crevasses are a constant hazard and the climbers are roped together in pairs to an experienced local guide for safety (see also page 141).

IF YOU get into trouble on a mountain can you be rescued by helicopter?

There is a small chance this may be possible, but all evacuation plans should be drawn up on the assumption that it isn't going to happen. Among the whole host of reasons:

- Mountainous regions have extremely unpredictable weather, with strong winds often swirling round the mountain itself— just the sort of conditions that may prevent a helicopter being able to get close.
- Helicopters have more trouble flying as the air gets thinner and provides less uplift for the rotor blades. The higher they go the less they can carry. Different types have different capabilities, and it may be that you are above the maximum altitude for local helicopters to fly—or to carry passengers.
- You could be so remote that there are simply no helicopters within flying range.
- In some countries a helicopter may not fly until the company gets a guarantee it's going to be paid. Air-worthiness is a whole other matter, but in a life-and-death situation you may feel checking the paperwork is not a priority.

Even if a helicopter does manage to come in it's unlikely to be able to land near a casualty. There may instead be a helicopter landing site lower down the mountain for emergency evacuations, and a casualty will need to be carried down to this point. This would prove to be no mean feat on some mountains where it's hard enough to get yourself down fully fit.

Glaciers and Snow

One of the great attractions of mountain climbing is to get above the snowline or onto a glacier. For many it's the natural world at its most stunning and awe-inspiring, but it can also, of course, be nature at its most lethal. Trekking or climbing in these surroundings requires special equipment and techniques. This is the territory of crampons, ice axes, harnesses, and ropes.

WALKING ON GLACIERS

Glaciers are made of solid ice (see page 23) and may be extremely steep, so walking up them would be all but impossible without crampons. These lightweight devices attach to climbing boots and usually have twelve sharp spikes to grip the ice. The idea is to get as many spikes as possible in contact with the glacier, and at first they can feel very awkward.

Walking down an incredibly steep, slippery glacier can be even more unnerving. Again, you need to get the maximum number of spikes into the ice. The Serious Andes expedition leader Ben Major describes the technique for doing this as "the diaper position." You walk down with your bottom pushed back into the slope as if you are wearing a soiled diaper.

For safety, climbers usually carry an ice axe on glaciers. If they slip and start to slide off the mountain they dig in the axe to stop themselves. Known as an ice axe arrest, it takes a lot of practice to ensure you don't end up skewering yourself, which would rather defeat the purpose.

Generally, climbers will also be roped together

WHAT HAPPENS IF you fall down a crevasse?

Being roped correctly to one or two companions might well be a lifesaver. The worst-case scenario is that you pull them in with you, but if they've practiced crevasse rescue drills that is unlikely. Hopefully, they'll be able to brace themselves and dig in their ice axes, which will then probably leave you dangling in space (if it's a deep crevasse). Not fun, but better than the alternative.

Obviously, the idea is to get you out as quickly as possible without putting other members of the expedition in danger. The rest of your rope team need to anchor the rope securely so they can untie themselves and figure out the best way to proceed.

Key to this is checking if you're injured while ensuring they don't end up falling in the crevasse (or in any others nearby, which might be hidden). There may occasionally be a simple solution, for example, lowering you a little to a shelf that leads back to safety, but otherwise they'll need to prepare a system for hauling you out. This can be very tricky—rescuers are operating on an icy glacier, quite possibly exhausted at high altitude, and the rope will be dug into the snow and ice at the edge of the crevasse. There are a whole host of crevasse rescue techniques which need to be learned.

with one or two companions, perhaps 10–15 m (30–50 ft) apart with the ropes kept reasonably taut. The exact distance is determined by the conditions and the state of the glacier. The rope team are responsible for each other's safety, especially if one of them falls down a crevasse.

CREVASSES

Glaciers are often full of deep cracks, called crevasses, formed along the "fault lines" where parts of the glacier are moving at different rates down the mountain. Crevasses are a great danger. They may be several yards across and hundreds of yards deep, and if the glacier is covered in snow they could be completely hidden.

Once again it's experienced local-guide time,

as they will know the areas on the glacier prone to crevasses and will try to plan a route to avoid them. Alternatively they may take snow "bridges" that are strong enough to cross over crevasses.

As a glacier is always on the move, new crevasses are opening up all the time. It's a constant battle of wits and there is no absolute guarantee of avoiding trouble.

SNOW SLOPES

Climbing on firm snow is similar to glacier travel, though in soft snow crampons can quickly clog up around the spikes (snowshoes may be a better option). Snow slopes may become treacherous as they warm up during the day and should always be assessed for avalanche risk.

Mountain Camps

Camping high up in some of the most spectacular locations on Earth is unforgettable, but it comes at a price:

- Everything you need has to be carried up there, which can be the last straw when struggling with the altitude.
- Conditions at the high altitude camp are unlikely to be ideal. It'll probably be freezing cold, and the wind may be so strong you lie awake all night fearing your tent's going to be blown away. The consolation is that the lack of oxygen means you probably wouldn't have slept much anyway.
- Far too many expeditions leave batteries, oxygen cylinders, and general trash on the pristine mountain slopes, turning them into giant garbage dumps. Try to live by the maxim: "What goes up, must come down!"

WHO NEEDS A TENT?

Some climbers prefer to try to avoid sleeping in a tent, particularly if they know the conditions up the mountain are likely to be good for snow caves. These are similar to igloos (see page 48), but hollowed out of packed snow in a deep drift. The site must be chosen carefully to minimize the risk of avalanche. Snow caves take quite a bit of effort to build but often feel a lot more secure—and infinitely quieter—than a tent vibrating and howling in a gale-force wind.

Perhaps the most extraordinary place to spend the night on a mountain is part of the way up a huge, vertical rock face. Dedicated rock climbers will tackle climbs of several days up sheer walls, sleeping in a portable cradle called a portaledge, which they attach to the rock (along with themselves of course). It's claimed that after an exhausting day on the rock face it can be very relaxing, but, dangling hundreds of yards up and relying on the bolts holding in the wall, it gives a whole new meaning to "falling asleep."

FOOD AND WATER

As on most expeditions, freeze-dried food is likely to be the order of the day, which at least means less load to carry up the mountain. Fresh food will go off and is too bulky. If you're lucky there may be a clean mountain stream as a water source, but at high altitude it may be a case of laboriously melting snow (see page 42). With so many other climbers likely to have been at the campsite before you it's hard to be sure the snow is clean, so water purification will be needed (see page 102).

Dehydration is a major problem when climbing. The cold, thin mountain air will have very little moisture in it (especially above the clouds), and you will probably be working far harder than normal. So you need to drink way more than you might expect.

HOW DO YOU camp on the side of a mountain?

Few mountains are shaped like the perfect volcanic cones you draw as a child, and so you can usually find flatter areas suitable for camping. As it happens, the volcano Cotopaxi tackled by the Serious Andes team is about as perfect a cone as you can get, sloping up at around 45˚. But once you get onto the mountain you realize that it too has less steep areas for resting and camping.

It's likely you'll find yourself sleeping on a bit of a slope, especially as comfort isn't top of the list when looking for a campsite. More critical is to avoid potential hazards like avalanches and rockfalls, and to get out of the worst of the wind. Sometimes it may be necessary to carve a flatter platform out of an ice or snow field.

Given the low temperatures and high winds, you'll want a similar sleeping system and windproof tent as for the Arctic (see page 48).

HOW DO YOU go to the bathroom on top of a mountain?

The problem is that with a limited number of good camping locations on a limited number of climbing routes, stunning mountain campsites are turning into glorified toilets covered in human waste.

The Serious Andes expedition decided that the "what goes up, must come down" principle should apply to human waste as well, so the agreed procedure was to poo into a plastic zip-up bag, either in the tent if alone, or behind the nearest rock. The bag was then deposited in a larger communal container to take back down the mountain.

There was a comedy moment when the container lid froze fast at 5,100 m (17,000 ft), and the expedition doctor decided the solution was to whack it on a rock. The cold, brittle container promptly smashed to bits, leaving a collection of unsavory plastic bags scattered in the snow. Fortunately, doctors are used to dealing with this kind of thing, and the "samples" were soon secure in two layers of trashbag.

Peeing needs to be separate to pooing (see Arctic Toilets, page 54), and should be in an agreed spot well away from any snow collection area.

Andean Horses

Stretching across much of the Andes mountain range above the treeline are "highland" areas known as Paramo or Altiplano. These inhospitable grasslands are found at altitudes between 3,000 m and 4,500 m (10,000 ft and 15,000 ft), and horses provide one of the few ways to get around.

Surrounded by high peaks, the feeling of freedom riding through the Andes has to be experienced to be believed (though for some Serious Andes adventurers this was over-ridden by the fear of riding up and down the steep slopes and through fast-flowing mountain streams).

To the untrained eye Andean horses appear to run wild across the hills, but nowadays many are actually kept within defined areas by deep trenches dug into the hillside. The horses, having been broken in (trained for riding) by the highly skilled local cowboys, are rounded up as and when they are needed.

COWBOY KIT

The weather in the Andean highlands is often extremely cold and wet, and the local cowboys have developed a style of clothing perfectly suited to the conditions. In Ecuador the cowboys are known as chagras and the key item in their kit is the poncho—traditionally either coarse llama wool or solid rubber—designed to keep the rain out and the heat of the horse in (as it rises from the horse's back).

Bottomless chaps, called zamarros, keep rain off the legs. Usually made of llama or goat skin, pairs for special occasions may be more

elaborate—made, for example, from bear or ocelot skin. Warm woollen scarves plus the obligatory cowboy hat complete the look. Cowboys aren't big on safety helmets, so if you're planning to ride in their territory it's advisable to take your own.

When riding for days up in the clouds, the ponchos are often preferred even by those who have access to modern Gore-Tex expedition clothing, as they believe the ponchos provide better protection from the fine, icy rain.

MOUNTAIN HORSES

Andean horses are thought to have been introduced from southern Spain in the fifteenth and sixteenth centuries after the Spanish conquest of South America. These Andalucian horses were relatively small and they evolved into hardy animals with long, thick coats to protect them from the harsh conditions at altitude.

Horses are ridden in Western style (rather than English), developed by cowboys for rounding up cattle. The rider doesn't bob up and down as much as in English style where more emphasis is placed on coinciding with the horse's movements.

The reins are much looser and held in one hand, pulled to one side or the other to tell the horse to change direction. There is a large pommel to hold onto at the front of the saddle and often large clog-like wooden stirrups to put the front of the feet in. These stirrups prevent the feet getting caught up in the long thick tufts of Paramo grass and also stop them getting soaked.

The expedition leaders Ben Major and Polly Murray in traditional llama and deer skin chaps (one of the young adventurers said Ben looked like a "gorilla-gram").

Mountain Peoples

When battling to conquer high peaks, lowland climbers will always face an uphill struggle—in every sense—compared with the world's mountain-dwelling peoples. Humans who've lived at high altitude for many generations have physically adapted to cope with the lack of oxygen in the air, in particular by developing bigger lungs. They're often described as having "barrel chests."

Interestingly, there are some key differences between mountain peoples in the Himalayas and in the Andes with regard to other adaptations to maximize the amount of oxygen. Tibetans and Sherpas in the Himalayas tend to have higher breathing rates than people who live at sea level, but a similar number of red blood cells (responsible for carrying oxygen round the body). For Andean tribespeople it's typically the reverse, with more red blood cells but a "normal" breathing rate.

LOW ALTITUDE SICKNESS

People living at altitude who come down to sea level can suffer a kind of reverse "low altitude" sickness. For instance, residents from Ecuador's capital Quito (2,800 m/9,300 ft) who head down to the coast for a tropical beach holiday may complain of headaches or feeling nauseous—until they acclimatize to taking in 50 percent more oxygen in each breath.

RECORD-BREAKING SHERPAS

The Sherpa are one of the native peoples of the Himalayas, but the name has become more well known in referring to the guides and porters (not all from the Sherpa tribe in fact) who help mountaineers climb the huge Himalayan peaks.

The Sherpas' ability to carry huge loads at great speed up mountains is legendary, and several have now gone into the Everest hall of

WHAT IS the highest that humans live?

Living for long periods of time above around 5,500 m (18,000 ft) is thought to be impossible for humans, as the body suffers continued physical deterioration with the lack of oxygen.

The highest known long-term human settlement was a sulphur-mining camp in the Chilean Andes at 5,300 m (17,500 ft), while thousands of people currently live at 5,100 m (17,000 ft) in the Peruvian Andes, mining for gold in terrible squalor and poverty at La Rinconada.

The people of Tibet, the "roof of the world," live permanently at altitudes up to around 5,000 m (16,700 ft).

Making a living at altitude is anything but "the high life." Conditions are extremely harsh and growing crops can be very tough, often needing terraces to be built into the hillside.

In the Andes, many mountain people are traditionally herders of llamas and alpacas, making clothes from the wool and using many other parts of the animals (see Andean Wildlife, page 120).

fame in their own right:

- In 2007, 47-year-old Appa Sherpa climbed Everest for an astonishing seventeenth time, breaking his own record for the most ascents.
- The record-holder for the fastest Everest ascent is Pemba Dorje Sherpa in an unbelievable 8 hrs 10 mins in 2004. It is so unbelievable, in fact, that it remains disputed, especially by Lhakpa Gelu Sherpa who believes he still holds the real record of 10 hours 56 mins, which he set in 2003. What is beyond dispute is that both climbers are phenomenal, as most expeditions take around four days.
- Babu Chiri Sherpa holds the record for time spent at the summit, camping overnight for more than 21 hours in 1999 (as if that weren't remarkable enough, he did it without extra oxygen). He sadly died on the mountain in 2001 after falling into a crevasse.
- The record for the youngest person to reach the summit is held by a female Sherpa. Ming Kipa Sherpa was fifteen when she climbed Everest in 2003. She had to tackle the mountain from the Tibetan side as Nepal doesn't allow attempts by climbers under the age of 16.
- And of course Tenzing Norgay Sherpa was first to conquer Everest with Sir Edmund Hillary in 1953.

TRADITIONAL FREEZE-DRIED FOOD

There comes a point on most expeditions when adventurers start to dream of fresh food instead of the freeze-dried stuff they inevitably have to eat day after day. What they probably don't realize is that Andean tribespeople have been freeze-drying potatoes and meat for centuries.

In an environment that may be hot during the day (in the sun) but well below freezing at night, they can, for example, naturally freeze-dry potatoes by repeatedly freezing them at night followed by thawing and removal of most of the moisture by day. The resulting freeze-dried potato, known as chuño, is extremely light for transportation and lasts for several years, a useful safeguard against harder times.

EATING GUINEA PIGS

Andean mountain people first started domesticating guinea pigs for food thousands of years ago, and the small rodents have remained a central part of their culture and diet. Many households breed guinea pigs in their kitchens purely for eating, often saving them for special occasions.

The creatures were a valuable food source well before they were kept as pets in other countries, so it's perhaps ironic that nowadays many pople find the idea of eating guinea pigs rather repulsive. A "treat" of barbecued guinea pig for the Serious Andes team caused quite a stir, but also led to the adventurers questioning their preconceived ideas about what meat is acceptable to eat and what is not.

Even when fully acclimated, lowland climbers
(left) will always struggle at altitude
compared with mountain-dwelling peoples.

Serious

THE HOSTILE DESERT

Lack of water and the unforgiving sun burning down from a cloudless sky make the desert seem hostile and unappealing to humans, but with the right planning it's not necessarily "hell on earth." In fact, the desert has some positive advantages over other extreme environments:

- It may be like an oven but at least it's a dry heat and much less unpleasant than the sticky humidity of a rainforest.
- Deserts usually have very cold nights, which means there's often a window of perfect weather to look forward to in the late afternoon as the day cools down (with another in the early morning as things start to heat up again).
- There are generally far fewer bugs flying around.

Desert

- Walking in sand dunes provides sensational, surreal views, which constantly change as the dunes shift and their shape alters in the breeze. When the wind drops the total silence in such a vast area is unreal.

During a long expedition, however, the seemingly endless landscape can become quite oppressive. The sand and dust get absolutely everywhere, and ensuring you have enough water to drink is a constant concern.

THE GREATEST DESERTS

The Sahara in North Africa is by far the world's largest desert (ignoring the cold desert of Antarctica), covering an area of around 9,000,000 sq km (3,500,000 sq miles), almost as much as the United States.

Flying south from Europe into Africa gives an idea of its enormous scale. For two hours you see nothing but desert below as you cover a distance of around 1,600 km (1,000 miles). Unlike the popular image only about one-third of the Sahara is made up of sand dunes, with vast gravel plains and mountainous regions making up the rest.

Second-biggest is the Arabian desert, less than one-third of the size of the Sahara at just under 2,500,000 sq km (1,000,000 sq miles). With possibly around two-thirds of the world's oil beneath the surface of the desert, it's an area which has seen great conflict.

The Gobi desert in Central Asia covers 1,300,000 sq km (500,000 sq miles). Spanning Mongolia and China, it was famously crossed by the Italian Marco Polo to reach China in 1275.

The Serious Desert Adventure

If the Serious Desert adventurers thought it never rained in the desert, their preconceptions were shattered almost immediately. As four-wheel drive vehicles took them to their training camp on the fringes of the Namib desert in Southern Africa, the heavens opened and the rain came down like it hadn't rained for years, which was quite possibly the case!

The sandy terrain was transformed into a quagmire; vehicle after vehicle got stuck and had to be pushed or towed out. A journey that was meant to take an hour turned into a five-hour marathon, with the worst awaiting them just as they approached the camp. Their route was blocked by a fast-flowing river, which hadn't existed just a few hours earlier.

The expedition leaders had to call their river-crossing techniques into play, something they hadn't expected in the desert (see Crossing Rivers, page 206). The river was still shallow enough to wade across but was rising rapidly. They had to move fast, stringing over a rope and crossing in threes, huddled together to resist the force of the water, which was surprisingly warm.

It was a dramatic start to an epic expedition. With more rain blighting training over the coming days, locals said it was the worst weather in the desert for thirty years.

The adventurers were going to attempt to walk 80 km (50 miles) across the Namib Desert to reach the infamous Skeleton Coast, using camels to carry their water and all other essentials. Their mission was to monitor and log details of rare desert rhinos along the way (see page 162). Before they set off they would also build a new enclosure for the camels.

ARE ALL deserts sandy?

Absolutely not. This is yet another of those misconceptions perpetuated by the movies and the media. Many desert areas are full of spectacular, barren mountainous terrain, while others are rather less appealing gravel-covered plains (looking rather like immense parking lots). Only about one-quarter of all deserts are made up of the classic sand dunes, which can be hundreds of feet high.

The World's Desert Regions

ARCTIC

Greenland

Siberia

NORTH
AMERICA

EUROPE

Great
Basin

Gobi
Desert

ASIA

Tropic of Cancer

Sahara Desert

Arabian
Desert

SOUTH EAST
ASIA

Atlantic
Ocean

AFRICA

Pacific
Ocean

Equator

SOUTH
AMERICA

Indian
Ocean

Tropic of Capricorn

Namib
Desert

AUSTRALIA

Australian
Desert

Kalahari
Desert

Pacific
Ocean

Patagonian
Desert

Southern
Ocean

The World's Desert Regions

desert regions

arid steppe regions

ANTARCTICA

To qualify as a desert an area must have very little rainfall,
generally agreed to be less than 25 cm (10 in) on average each
year. Deserts are also very barren with almost no vegetation.

While in training they slept in traditional mud huts, which were not to everyone's taste because of the large number of bugs that lived in the thatched roof and were prone to drop down on the occupants. But larger creatures were a much greater concern. The camp was in lion and elephant territory, and for safety nobody was allowed out of the huts at night. Pee bottles were provided, with extra large funnels for the girls.

The scale of what they were taking on was highlighted by a short training trek of just 5 km (3 miles) to camp out in the desert for the night. On the main expedition they would need to trek for eight hours each day, but within fifteen minutes of setting off in temperatures of 38°C (100°F) several of the team were suffering badly in the heat.

They slept by a dune under a tarpaulin lean-to, and to keep lions away each had to take an hour on sentry duty by a fire through the night. Several were spooked by rustling sounds in the pitch black beyond the camp fire, which usually turned out to be nothing more than one of the film crew moving about.

The team slowly got fitter and began to acclimatize to the intense heat, but their camel enclosure project was still to prove a huge challenge. They had undertaken to complete the whole thing in just three days on the promise of a unique treat at the end. But it was very tough laboring under the burning subtropical sun. One of the young adventurers commented he'd rather be in geography class.

The project reached crisis point on the final evening as it became clear there was an extremely late night in store. By midnight the team was on its knees having toiled for around 15 hours—but the work still wasn't finished. In a superhuman triumph of mind over matter, the adventurers forced themselves to go on right through the night. They made it to the official opening on absolutely no sleep, and four camels duly loped into the completed enclosure right on schedule.

The reward was an extraordinary trip for the entire team away from the desert to a game

The Serious Desert team cross rivers formed just hours earlier in a rare desert downpour.

reserve called Ongava, to help in the darting of rhinos by helicopter. The white rhinos were getting a check-up and having their horns fitted with microchips to deter poachers. The adventurers took part in the whole process: one rode in the helicopter, others kept the darted rhinos cool, drilled the valuable horns, and even stuck thermometers up the rhinos' behinds to take their temperature—truly a once-in-a-lifetime experience!

For their main marathon mission the team were tracking even rarer black rhinos in the desert. With six camels in tow to carry supplies and water, they had six days to monitor rhinos and walk the 80 km (50 miles) to the Skeleton Coast.

Only about a hundred and fifty desert-adapted black rhinos are left, spread over a vast area, so the adventurers were relying on local knowledge of the few waterholes where the rhinos tend to hang out. Unfortunately, there was a major hitch. With the freak rainstorms of the previous few weeks the huge animals were in the luxurious position of being able to roam almost wherever they pleased and still find water.

The adventurers trekked for three days in 40°C (104°F) heat without finding any rhino. Every time they got on the trail of one, its tracks eventually showed it had raced off well before they got close. Morale plummeted, especially as the team were starting to suffer from bad blisters, headaches, and sheer exhaustion. They were covering around 16 km (10 miles) a day and every night was still disturbed by an hour of sentry duty.

On the final day before they hit the rhino-free dune belt they finally tracked down a rhino sitting peacefully in the sun. As they noted all its details there was a heart-stopping moment. The huge animal got to its feet and looked directly at them. With phenomenal hearing and sense of smell, was he feeling under threat and about to charge? Fortunately, the one-and-a-half-ton rhino turned tail and raced off in a cloud of dust at an incredible 48 km/h (30 mph).

Although they'd hoped to see far more rhinos, they now had to turn their attention to getting

The adventurers lead the camels through mile after mile of dry riverbed in their search for rare black rhino.

A helicopter completes the darting of a white rhino, which is silhouetted between the trees amid clouds of dust thrown up by the rotors.

EXPEDITION LOCATION

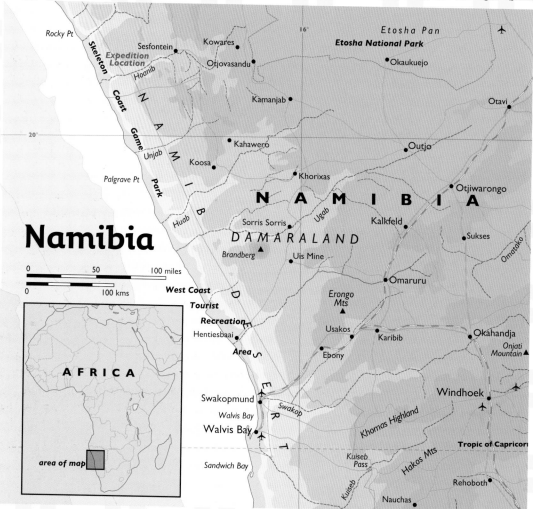

Namibia

0   50   100 miles

0   100 kms

AFRICA

area of map

Rocky Pt

Skeleton Coast

Expedition Location

Sesfontein

Kowares

Otjovasandu

Kamanjab

Kahawero

Koosa

Khorixas

Etosha Pan

Etosha National Park

Okaukuejo

Otavi

Outjo

Otjiwarongo

Hoanib

Unjab

Palgrave Pt

Game Park

Huab

Sorris Sorris

Ugab

Brandberg ▲

Uis Mine

N A M I B I A

D A M A R A L A N D

Kalkfeld

Sukses

Omatako

Omaruru

Erongo Mts

West Coast Tourist Recreation Area

Hentiesbaai

Usakos

Karibib

Ebony

Okahandja

Onjati Mountain ▲

Swakopmund

Walvis Bay

Walvis Bay

Swakop

Windhoek

Khomas Highland

Tropic of Capricorn

Sandwich Bay

Kuiseb Pass

Hakos Mts

Kuiseb

Nauchas

Rehoboth

The Namib desert is made up of a variety of terrains, ranging from flat sandy plains to spectacular, rugged mountains.

through the treacherous sand dunes which stood between them and the Skeleton Coast.

Walking on loose sand was draining and the team had to double back constantly as routes proved too difficult for the camels. The weather was getting cooler and cooler as they got nearer to the coast, and a night camping out in the dunes proved absolutely freezing. They awoke soaking wet, covered in dew.

Frustratingly, even when they caught a tantalizing glimpse of the sea from the top of a dune, they had to keep heading away from the coast to find a route through. But finally, after six days and more than 80 km (50 miles) of trekking through some of the most hostile desert on Earth they finally made it to the Skeleton Coast, a towering achievement for the young team.

THE NAMIB DESERT AND THE SKELETON COAST

The Serious Desert expedition took place in the Namib, one of two deserts in the sparsely populated Southern African country of Namibia. The total population is just two million in an area more than three times the size of the UK.

The Namib is often described as the oldest desert in the world and borders the Skeleton Coast, notorious for its thick fogs. The beaches are littered with the wrecks of boats that lost their way and ran onto rocks. The coast takes its name from the bones of the many unfortunate sailors who survived the initial shipwreck only to perish in the barren desert conditions they were then confronted with.

The fog comes about because of the uncharacteristically cold Atlantic waters for the subtropical latitude. Ocean currents sweep ice-cold water up from the Antarctic, and the meeting of warm air and the cold ocean leads to frequent fog.

This weather pattern is also a major factor in the formation of the Namib desert itself, as the lack of evaporation from the cold water means there is little rain.

Like many deserts, the Namib is made up of a variety of terrains, with the adventurers first encountering flat sandy plains surrounded by spectacular, rugged mountains. They also walked through gravel plains and finally had to cross the sand dune belt that runs parallel to the Skeleton Coast.

The Skeleton Coast is flanked by a desert dune belt, which formed an impenetrable barrier to many a shipwrecked sailor.

Desert Wildlife

You might be forgiven for imagining there is absolutely no wildlife in the desert. What could possibly survive in such extreme temperatures with so little water and vegetation? Well, the answer is that once again nature has done an extraordinary job of evolving to cope with the harshest conditions, and specially adapted mammals, reptiles, insects, and birds are all found in the desert.

Desert animals have developed some fiendishly clever ways of coping with the heat and lack of water, none more so than the domesticated creature most associated with the desert—the camel (see page 166).

One of the best safeguards against the extreme heat is to be nocturnal. Many desert animals hide from the burning sun by day and only come out during the cooler evening and night.

In Namibia's Namib desert, where the Serious Desert expedition took place, the lifeline for many animals is the fog that drifts in off the cold ocean on many mornings. Extracting a few precious drops of moisture from the fog is crucial. It may be all the water some creatures get all day.

LONG-LEGGED BEETLE

Unique to the Namib, this beetle climbs to the top of a dune at dawn to collect droplets from the fog. It uses its hind legs to push its bottom end up so the drops collect on its body and trickle down special grooves into its mouth.

In another adaptation the beetle has also developed long legs—and even special hairs at the bottom of its legs—to make it taller so its body is a critical extra distance from the red-hot sand.

SIDEWINDER

Sidewinder snakes are common to many deserts. As the name suggests they've developed a sideways, winding movement to cross the sand,

Long-legged beetles push their bottom ends up towards the damp coastal fog drifting inland over the Namib desert.

which means only a small part of the body is in contact with the burning hot surface at any point.

Two small species of sidewinder live in the Namib desert. Both are venomous vipers, around 30 cm (1 ft) in length. In the early morning they curl up in the fog and lick the moisture off their body. As the day heats up the snakes can quickly bury themselves in the sand to get out of the sun, leaving just eyes and nostrils visible. Here they lie in wait—possibly for weeks—to ambush their prey, feeding mainly on small lizards. Their bites are painful to humans, but rarely fatal.

Scorpions are also found in the desert but are again not usually deadly. Young children and the elderly are at greatest risk (see Dangerous Creatures, page 82).

ORYX

Also known as a gemsbok, this large type of antelope is found wandering deep into the Namib from semi-arid areas on the fringes of the desert. A national symbol of Namibia, the oryx is notable for its two beautiful straight horns. The spear-like horns are lethal weapons, lowered in defense against attacks by predators such as lions. It has the lightest-colored coat of all antelopes in order to reflect sunlight, and it can breathe very fast to help cool down, panting like a dog.

The oryx also allows its body temperature to rise far higher than most other mammals (up to around 45°C (113°F), which would be fatal for most) with a specially adapted blood-circulation system to cool the blood before it gets to the brain.

Like many desert-adapted animals, the oryx gets much of its moisture from rugged desert plants, and can also use its front teeth to dig for roots and water under the surface.

Many other mammals, including hyenas, lions, and giraffe are also found roaming the desert, but will generally return more often than the oryx to slightly less arid areas.

OSTRICH

Not only is the ostrich the largest and heaviest of all birds, it's also the fastest runner, reaching remarkable speeds of over 64 km/h (40 mph). This flightless bird is taller than a human at 2.5 m (8 ft), and is also heavier than most people at around a 100 kg (220 lbs). Found in many arid areas of Africa, it's well adapted to life in the desert, able
to live for long periods when dehydrated and using its thick plumage to insulate its body from the sun. Like the oryx, it pants rapidly to cool down if necessary.

HAIRY-FOOTED GERBIL

This stocky gerbil spends its day in a complex network of underground burrows to avoid the heat, emerging at night to search for seeds, leaves, and insects. Other small mammals have similar lifestyles, including mice and moles. Although gerbils are occasionally found in the sand dunes, like most mammals they generally live away from the dunes in other parts of the desert.

DESERT ELEPHANTS AND RHINOS

The Namib desert is famous for its unique populations of desert-adapted elephants and black rhinos. Both creatures can go three or four days without water (far longer than their non-adapted cousins). They generally live in and around the more fertile dry riverbeds, or wadis, as they are known, and are adapted to travel vast distances in search of waterholes.

Desert elephants use tusks, trunk, and feet to dig deep trenches to locate water, and both creatures appear to pass on down the generations the knowledge of where water can be found.

The desert elephant feeds on a wide range of plants and grasses. The black rhino is also able to feed on most desert plants, its favorite being the euphorbia bush, which is in fact highly toxic to many other species including humans. Even brushing against the bush can cause extreme irritation, and getting the sap in your eye can cause blindness.

Around six hundred specially adapted elephants live in the arid Namib desert.

THREATS TO DESERT ELEPHANTS AND RHINOS

The populations of both species were on the brink of extinction twenty years ago after savage poaching for horns and tusks. With fewer than four hundred elephants and just seventy rhino left, drastic action was taken to halt the slaughter.

The Namibian charity Save the Rhino Trust (SRT) was instrumental in patrolling the inhospitable areas and protecting the endangered animals. In one of the great success stories of wildlife conservation, the populations are slowly recovering. The number of desert elephants has passed six hundred and there are now about one hundred and fifty black rhino.

A rare desert-adapted black rhino rests in the heat of the day.

THE SERIOUS DESERT RHINO TRACKING PROJECT

SRT regularly patrols the Namib to monitor the population of desert-adapted rhinos, keeping tabs on their health and location to help protect them from disease and poaching.

The Serious Desert team trekked with camels into some of the most remote areas of the desert to help track down rhinos and contribute to the SRT database.

WHY DO elephants and rhinos live in the desert?

It does perhaps seem strange that they should have ended up in such a hostile environment, but there are countless other examples of creatures—including humans—who've adapted to environments that initially seem far from ideal.

We can only speculate about the reasons elephants and rhinos started to populate the desert. Before the animals were endangered there may well have been large numbers competing for limited resources in less arid areas, and the desert regions could have offered a better chance of survival to those who could cope with the harsh conditions.

Now they are established and adapted to the area there is no reason to move away. If the populations were to die out their unique knowledge of the area would die with them and the animals would never return, at least until evolution possibly did its thing again in millions of years time.

DESERT TRICKS

Other creatures also have some extraordinary party tricks to cope with life in the desert:

- The Namib golden wheel spider is an acrobat, avoiding predators and saving energy by forming its eight legs into a circle and cartwheeling down sand dunes.
- Some lizards can dive head first into the sand at full speed and bury themselves if chased by predators.
- In a mesmerising desert "dance," several lizards raise diagonally opposite feet off the hot sand to cool them. They lift front right and back left feet, then a few seconds later lower them and lift the front left and back right.

DESERT PLANTS

Many desert animals rely on the fact that plants have also managed to adapt and live in the hostile conditions.

- Cacti are always first to be associated with the desert for very good reason, with extremely efficient ways of cutting down water loss including no conventional leaves or stems. Their rounded shape maximizes the amount of water stored while minimizing the surface area from which water evaporates.
- Many desert plants have extremely deep root systems to find water lying well below the surface.
- Some seeds can lie dormant for long periods until a heavy rainstorm produces favorable conditions—and magically, land barren for years suddenly turns green.

Desert Clothing

Think of dressing for the oven and the fridge—and the very occasional sand-blasting and shower—and you won't go far wrong in the desert. Temperatures by day can reach 50°C (122°F), while at night they may plummet to around freezing point—a result of the clear skies and extremely dry air.

The lack of humidity means that unlike the rainforest you can wear slightly heavier clothing such as cotton (in a humid jungle it would be almost instantly soaked and stuck to you). This is useful for protecting you from the burning sun and keeping you warmer at night.

To protect you from the sun, always wear a long-sleeved shirt, long pants, and a hat and apply high-factor sunscreen. Light-colored clothing is best for reflecting sunlight.

Not only is sunburn extremely painful, it will leave you feeling even hotter—all in all the last thing you need when you're already struggling with the conditions.

CLOTHING CHECKLIST

- Wide-brimmed hat with ventilation holes
- Good quality wrap-around sunglasses
- Light-colored, long-sleeved cotton shirt
- Cotton pants
- Loose-fitting clothes are much more comfortable
- Desert boots with thick soles and canvas tops allow feet to breathe. To avoid blisters these must be well worn-in before hiking in the desert.
- A light rainproof jacket is useful in case of rare downpours, and a fleece will be needed for the evening. Even thermal underwear might be necessary in some deserts.

Trekking down a dry riverbed in search of the rare desert rhino.

HOW DO YOU keep the sand out of your eyes?

In light breezes wrap-around sunglasses should do the trick, while goggles may be useful if the wind gets up. For full-blown sandstorms the only answer is to sit it out. Take shelter if possible, or huddle up with your back to the wind and cover up completely, placing a handkerchief or similar over your mouth and nose. Any exposed flesh will literally be sand-blasted, another reason to avoid shorts and T-shirts.

SANDSTORMS

When strong winds get up in sandy deserts they may pick up so much sand that it forms vast clouds, reducing visibility to near zero. In certain weather conditions the sandstorm may be up to a mile high and its approach can be an awesome (and rather scary) sight.

After the storm has passed through, the entire appearance of the area may be changed, with dunes having shifted location and reformed in different shapes.

Worryingly, some areas are reporting more frequent and intense sandstorms. In the Gobi desert recent sandstorms have been known to last for a week.

A huge sandstorm sweeps across the Namib desert, changing the entire appearance of the area.

Camels

Sometimes referred to as the "ships of the desert," camels are the very symbol of desert life. These supreme desert creatures have served humankind for centuries, though they are not always the easiest animals to work with. They can be smelly, stubborn, and not particularly affectionate (though camel handlers talk of a bond greater than that between a horse and its owner).

The Serious Desert expedition leader, Bruce Parry, put it succinctly: "They snort, they fart, they emit noxious fumes. It's just normal—they're camels." Soon after, one showed its displeasure at an attempt to put a bridle over its head by spitting foul-smelling, vomit-like saliva straight in the eye of one of the adventurers.

TYPES OF CAMEL

There are two main species of camel: the single-humped Arabian camel—or dromedary—and the double-humped Bactrian camel (as well as the South American members of the camel family—see Andean wildlife, page 120).

The Bactrian camel is most at home in rocky, cooler deserts, while the Arabian camel has a whole host of remarkable adaptations to enable it to survive in the harshest desert conditions:

- Its body temperature is able to rise to levels that would kill most other mammals (a similar trick to the oryx—see page 159).
- To conserve water it doesn't sweat until its body temperature reaches its upper limit of around 41°C (106°F).
- It copes with severe dehydration, losing up to one-quarter of its body weight without harm (humans have problems losing five per cent).
- In hard times it relies on the fat stored in its hump, which then slumps over or disappears completely. The hump is not a water store as commonly believed.
- If necessary, it can eat thorny plants and dry leaves avoided by other animals.
- Its nostrils can be completely closed to keep out sand.
- Its long eyelashes also keep out sand.

The Serious Desert team trekked across the Namib desert with six camels carrying all their camping equipment, food, and water.

- A soft pad between two of its toes spreads out when the foot goes down to help gain traction when walking on sand.
- A hard calloused area on the knees allows the animal to kneel on the red-hot sand.

CAMEL TRAINS

For thousands of years camels have been used to transport goods across the desert. An Arabian camel can carry around 150 kg (300 lbs), a stockier Bactrian camel twice as much.

RIDING CAMELS

A well trained camel can be ridden in much the same way as a horse, and can gallop at speeds of up to 64 km/h (40 mph).

There are common commands given to camels when leading or riding them. These are usually accompanied by a firm tug on the reins in the required direction.

"Cush" instructs the camel to lie down (important so its load can be strapped on), while "up" should get it back up again. Many other instructions are similar to those used by husky dog mushers (see page 40), such as "haw" for turning left and "jee" for right.

HOBBLING

This widespread practice is a way of restraining camels so they can't wander too far. Hobbling involves tying one of the camel's front legs so it's bent over double at the knee; the camel then has to "hobble" around on three legs.

To some it may look uncomfortable and cruel, but the practice has been used for generations and does not seem to particularly worry the animals. Building the Serious Desert enclosure meant camels using it would no longer have to be hobbled.

 HOW LONG can a camel go without water?

On expedition, fully laden camels have been known to go for up to a week without food or water, so a few days is no problem at all. When not carrying a load they can manage without drinking for months, relying on just the moisture in food.

ARABIAN CAMEL	BACTRIAN CAMEL
One hump	Two humps
Found from North Africa to Northern India	Found in Central Asia
Adapted to hot, sandy deserts	Adapted to rockier, cooler deserts
2 m (7 ft) tall to top of hump	Slightly shorter and stockier with a darker coat
Short, thick wool	Longer, finer wool
Domesticated and not found in the wild	Mainly domesticated but a few thousand still in the wild

Crossing the Desert

Before heading into a desert it's useful to be a bit of a mathematician. How many days will the journey take? How much water will you need? How much does it weigh? What about fuel and food? And crucially, have you factored in contingency plans for worst-case scenarios? Sandstorms can pin you down for hours and disorientate you, while rainstorms can bog you down and slow progress dramatically, even making planned routes impassable.

WALKING WITH CAMELS

Given how heavy water is and that the camels will be carrying it, the calculations of how much will be needed for the journey are critical. This will depend on whether there are guaranteed places to fill up along the way. And while camels can go for days without water, sooner or later they'll also need to be able to top up.

Only when you've figured all this out will you be able to decide exactly how many camels you need on your expedition and how best to spread the load, which will also include food and camping equipment.

To save weight, people usually walk alongside the camel train rather than riding, though one or two camels may be given a relatively light load in case someone falls ill and needs a ride.

Most expeditions plan to move in the early morning and late afternoon, resting in the heat of the day—in shade if possible.

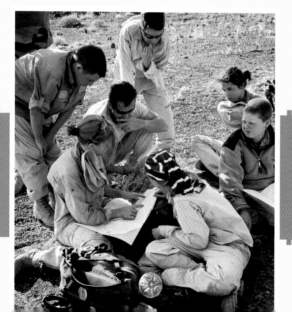

An early morning snooze before a long day hiking in the dunes.

DRIVING IN DESERTS

This is about as far from driving down the average motorway as it's possible to get: no gas stations, no services, no tow trucks, no other vehicles for days on end (if at all), and often no actual road.

If at all feasible it's always far better to travel as a party of at least two vehicles. One can tow the other out if stuck; and in the event of a serious breakdown there's still a way out.

There's a fairly obvious checklist of lifesaving precautions if you are about to drive into the desert (though it's remarkable how many folk don't follow the most basic safety measures):

- Use only the most reliable, recently serviced four-wheel drives
- Ensure drivers are well qualified in off-road driving
- Drivers need to be able to carry out basic repairs
- Basic spare parts and engine fluids should be carried
- Make sure there's more than enough fuel and water
- Take a GPS handset for navigation and a satellite phone for emergency communication
- Don't forget the tow rope and shovel, and, ideally, planks or metal runners to put in front of wheels if stuck in sand
- Tell someone of your plans

A Serious Desert camp in the Namib desert. The tarpaulin lean-to was secured by attaching the guy ropes to bags filled with sand (not exactly in short supply).

DRY RIVERBEDS

You often hear of dry riverbeds in desert regions. These are generally not seasonal rivers, which crop up during the rainy season elsewhere in the tropics, but drainage channels that only turn briefly into rivers after rare, heavy desert rainstorms.

Also known as ephemeral rivers or wadis, they usually disappear within hours or days at most. The riverbeds are more fertile than the surrounding desert, with occasional waterholes and more vegetation, making them favored locations for desert creatures.

While they can be good routes for walking or driving through, you really need to know your desert. They may have sheer sides with no way out for mile after mile, and a freak rainstorm some distance away could send a flash flood crashing though without warning.

Also, some deserts have restrictions on where you are allowed to drive. For example, in areas of the Namib, vehicles have to keep to set routes and are forbidden from driving down most wadis, as the vehicle tracks may remain for generations.

 DOES IT ever rain in the desert?

Does it ever! Ask the Serious Desert team, whose introduction to the Namib desert was pushing vehicles out of the mud and wading through torrents in the pouring rain (see page 152).

But it was said to be the worst weather in years, and that's really the point. Deserts are very unpredictable. They can go for years without rain and then get a downpour worthy of a rainforest.

The overall desert average of less than 25 cm (10 in) per year may all come in a few hours.

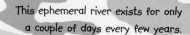
This ephemeral river exists for only a couple of days every few years.

HOW DO YOU sleep safely in elephant and lion territory?

Thankfully tents look like impenetrable barriers to a lion or elephant. The animals don't seem to realize that they could easily break them down, and an elephant will always avoid stepping on a tent except when in a blind panic.

The key problem is leaving the tent in the night. If an elephant has wandered into camp, it could be completely freaked out by your sudden appearance and might crush you. So it's best to arrange to pee in the tent if possible.

If sleeping in the open or under a tarpaulin, a watch system through the night by the campfire is the answer, as lions and elephants won't come near a fire where there are people moving and talking. Even so, it's essential to have an experienced armed guide on hand at all times while in wild animal territory.

Guides should also advise on where to make camp, avoiding well used animal tracks and areas near waterholes.

DESERT CAMPS

There's quite a choice of how to sleep for the night in the desert. You could simply go for a standard tent, you could sleep under a tarpaulin lean-to by a dune, or you could even sleep out in the open under the amazingly clear, black sky filled with brilliant stars.

A warm sleeping system will be needed as the temperature may well plummet. If not under canvas this may, surprisingly, also need to be fully waterproof. This is not just to cover the rare rainstorm; as you get nearer the Skeleton Coast in the Namib, for example, the early morning fogs drifting in off the sea leave everything dripping wet.

Water, Water!

The basic cartoon image is always the same—a disheveled man crawling on his knees through the sand in the burning sun, dying of thirst and calling out, "Water, water!" It's an image that has launched a thousand jokes and, of course, part of the humor lies in the fact that it describes a deadly serious situation. Without water in the desert an adult would last a couple of days at most, far less if using up lots of energy trying to reach safety.

As with other very hot environments like the jungle, it's vital to keep taking in water constantly to avoid dehydration. A useful guide is that you should never actually feel thirsty, as it indicates you're probably already starting to get dehydrated.

For a long expedition you—or your camels—are unlikely to be able to carry all the water you need, so the journey will need to be planned with waterholes or springs in mind for refilling, following the usual purification regime of iodine drops or boiling.

FINDING WATER

There is no substitute for the knowledge of local guides as to where water can be found in the desert, but in an emergency, animals may be the best guide available. Follow animal tracks or watch out for where

CAN YOU drink your own pee?

There are two different issues here: a) "Will drinking your own urine do you any harm?" and b) "Will drinking urine actually help if you're dying of thirst?"

In answer to the first question, when your pee first comes out of your body it is fairly sterile (in other words has no harmful bacteria). Although it contains lots of chemicals rejected by your body it's unlikely to do you any harm to drink a small amount. In fact, throughout history some groups and religions have promoted drinking urine as a cure for various illnesses - completely unproven scientifically it has to be said. (Note that

they only recommend absolutely "fresh" urine. Once it's out of the body bacteria get to work on it very quickly which is why it soon starts to smell.)

Now, as for resorting to drinking urine in the absence of water, it's not really going to help much. Firstly, with a high salt content the body would use vital fluid trying to get rid of it again; and secondly, you'd be so dehydrated by this point that you would produce very little urine anyway.

Having said that, there are a few famous survival tales where adventurers in dire situations believe sipping urine helped prolong their life long enough to be rescued.

TURNING URINE INTO WATER

The Serious Desert team conducted an experiment as part of desert training to see if a special kind of solar still could be used in emergency to extract water from urine.

It required two wide-bodied plastic bottles with small necks. Having peed into one, the two bottles were carefully taped together. The theory was that by placing the pee bottle in the sun and the collection bottle in the shade, pure water would be produced.

A few hours after setting up the bottles, a little water had indeed collected. The adventurers tentatively sipped it and most found it absolutely fine. Unfortunately, one boy said that his "sample" tasted rather like, well, urine—it transpired that he'd not been very careful separating the two bottles and some wee had probably got into the purified water.

Although the method was shown to work, a whole series of bottles—and lots of urine—would be needed to produce a signifi-cant amount of water in a genuine emergency. Depending on equipment available, a solar still might be more practical (see over).

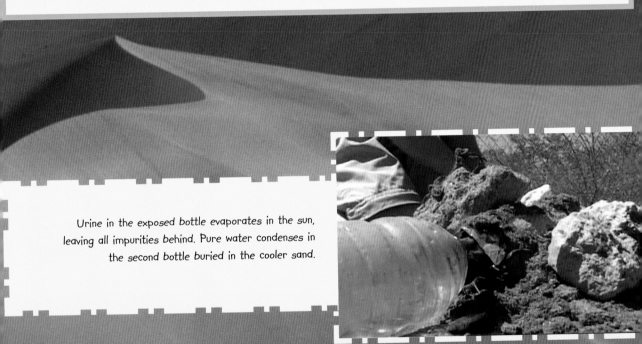

Urine in the exposed bottle evaporates in the sun, leaving all impurities behind. Pure water condenses in the second bottle buried in the cooler sand.

birds are gathering at dawn and dusk. (This does not apply to vultures, though, as they may be simply circling over a carcase).

Failing that, your options are diminishing rapidly but there are still a few things to try:

- Various ways can be devised to collect the morning fog in the Namib desert, making use of tarpaulins, vehicle surfaces, or foliage. It may be as simple as mopping it up with a cloth and squeezing out the moisture.
- Crevices in rocks may fill with water, and can be tapped using a straw or drinking tube.
- Some cacti have "juice" inside them, like the barrel cactus found in American deserts. The liquid is not actually sloshing around inside, so you can't just poke a straw through as in the cartoons. It's obtained by cutting the top off the cactus (far easier said than done—there are sharp spikes everywhere), and squeezing the cloudy liquid out of the fleshy pulp inside. It doesn't taste great but may be the difference between life and death.

The key problem is identifying the right species. Confusingly most plants with milky sap are to be avoided as they are poisonous (and in the Namib desert the euphorbia, as favored by desert rhinos, is one of most poisonous plants known to humans).

MAKING A SOLAR STILL

If there is any moisture at all in the ground a solar still can be used to collect it. As the air in the hole heats up, water evaporates from the sand or soil and condenses on the underside of the plastic sheet, running into the container. You can also introduce moisture by peeing into the still (carefully avoiding the container of course), or by putting in any available green leaves.

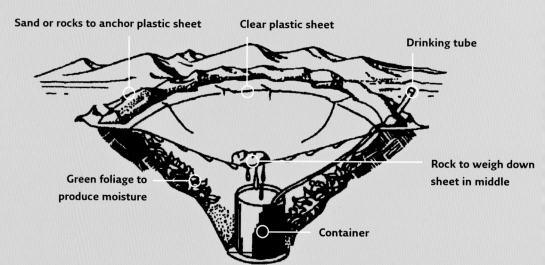

Sand or rocks to anchor plastic sheet

Clear plastic sheet

Drinking tube

Rock to weigh down sheet in middle

Green foliage to produce moisture

Container

The Extreme Desert team prepare to spend the night in the dunes of the Namib desert.

Animal Tracking

It is always hugely impressive—and often quite mystifying—to see how expert local trackers can get on the trail of a wild animal. They are attuned to tiny signs that most of us would not even notice, let alone be able to interpret. Animal tracking skills have been passed on down the generations, and although originally developed by hunters looking for food they are increasingly employed nowadays to help find and view ever-scarcer wildlife.

ANIMAL DETECTIVES

The ability to piece together the tiniest clues comes with experience, usually after years of living on the land. There are a whole host of different telltale signs to the trained eye, which together can give a remarkably detailed picture of the recent behavior and location of the animal.

1) Tracks

Animal footprints can reveal a whole range of information, and not just the obvious such as type of animal and the direction it's traveling. A good tracker may also be able to tell:

- The size of the animal.
- The speed it was traveling—toes will usually be more dug in if running, and the pattern of prints may be different for different gaits.
- How long ago the animal passed through - for example, the older the tracks in the desert, the more sand may be blown in.

2) Poo

Smelling droppings and pulling apart piles of dung may seem an odd way to earn a living, but poo really is a remarkably rich source of animal data:

- The temperature of the poo and how moist it is tells trackers how long ago the animal was around doing its business.
- In the absence of clear tracks, the shape and texture of the poo may identify the animal, and this can be confirmed by examining its

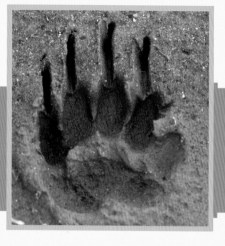

Look for the five toes and large pad to detect a badger's prints.

Otters are usually found near a river. Their pads are almost round.

contents. Bits of bone and feathers indicate a carnivore, while nuts and seeds point to a herbivore.

- Animal researchers also analyze the content of poo to learn about the animal's diet, health, and behavior. (Note that dung is often full of harmful organisms, so disposable gloves should always be worn).

3) Food remains

The trail of nut shells and bits of fruit left by an animal is clear as day to an expert eye:

- The type of food may itself be a giveaway to a local tracker who knows the animals in the area.
- Different animals have different ways of getting nuts from shells. The shell may, for example, have been gnawed, pecked open, or split in two, and teeth marks may be visible.

4) Dens, rubbings, and other signs:

- The discovery of an animal den or sleeping area usually provides positive identification of the animal.

- Bits of fur or feathers may be left accidentally when the animal passes a sharp branch or rough bark.
- Some animals rub against a tree deliberately, perhaps to scratch themselves, leaving distinctive markings.
- Top trackers can spot the faintest differences in texture of a surface, indicating something has walked over it. For instance, getting down to surface level at dawn may highlight slight variations in the shine of the dew where an animal has stepped, or they may spot that blades of grass are slightly disturbed.

IDENTIFYING ANIMAL TRACKS

The tracks themselves are of course often a lot less perfect than what you see in a textbook, especially if the soil or sand is fairly dry, and it takes some practice to distinguish between different species. For example, below are the tracks of some animals which might be found in more temperate regions such as the UK.

Deer prints are distinctive mainly because they have just two toes.

Fox prints are often confused with those of dogs.

-WHAT DO YOU DO if a rhino charges at you?

A ton and a half of wild animal charging at you at 48 km/h (30 mph) is definitely one of the scarier experiences in life. This was a very real concern in the planning of Serious Desert, where the team were actively tracking desert rhino in dry riverbeds and on open plains.

Unfortunately, every rhino expert seemed to have their own answer to the question. This is perhaps indicative that in real emergencies the correct course of action depends on the particular circumstances, which will rarely be exactly the same.

Rhinos have poor eyesight but remarkably acute hearing and sense of smell, so they should always be approached silently from downwind. Simply being on the ground 50 m (163 ft) from a rhino gets the heart racing, and if at all possible it's wise to be right next to a vehicle you can instantly leap aboard. Failing that, large trees to duck behind are reassuring, though of course in the desert they are few and far between.

Attempting to run away is futile as rhinos are far too fast. Because of their great bulk they are, however, not so adept at sharp turns once they're in full flight, so some survival experts recommend standing your ground until the last moment and then leaping off to the side (perhaps not one to rely on unless completely out of other options). Although you would hope never to resort to it, your life may ultimately depend on a trained marksman who should accompany the expedition at all times. This will often be an experienced ex-hunter as it's rather important they won't panic at the crucial moment. The marksman will need to stand over to the side of the party as it's hard to get in a fatal shot head-on.

- GPS COLLARS

Research into animal behavior has been transformed in recent years by the latest satellite equipment. Attaching a GPS collar to the animal (usually when it's sedated) allows animal researchers and game wardens to learn about the exact routes it takes, how far it roams, and, of course, where it is at any given point.

Most GPS collars will store the details of the animal's movements and periodically download the information via a satellite, or locally to a computer.

Much cheaper—but also much more limited—is the radio collar. This simply sends out a signal that a researcher can pick up from up to a couple of miles away, allowing the animal to be located.

A lion leaves its tracks across the Namib desert.

Desert Peoples

Like the Inuit of the Arctic "cold desert," the peoples who live in the world's hot deserts have adapted to some of the most demanding conditions known to humans. Most desert peoples live a nomadic existence, traveling from area to area in search of food and water. This has shaped their lifestyles, with very few possessions and great reliance on camels where they exist, or the ability to walk vast distances where they do not. Two prime examples are the Bedouin tribespeople of the Sahara and Middle Eastern deserts, and the San people of the Kalahari in Southern Africa.

THE BEDOUIN

Traditionally, the Arabic-speaking Bedouin are nomadic animal herders, keeping goats, sheep, or camels on whatever grazing land they can find, moving on as it becomes exhausted.

Bedouins wear loose-fitting robes and headgear, which cover up their entire body apart from the face. Long experience tells them it's cooler than exposing more flesh to the burning sun, and it also protects against wind and sand.

Camels are central to Bedouin life. As well as a beast of burden carrying possessions across the desert, the camel provides milk and meat, its dung is used for fuel, and its hair for tents and clothing.

Though often extremely poor, the tribespeople are renowned for their hospitality. It is a very important part of their culture to welcome strangers and put them up in their tents.

Over the past fifty years many Bedouins have moved to "civiliztion," some forced off their land, others in search of an easier lifestyle. Fewer than one-tenth of all Bedouins are now thought to lead a truly nomadic life.

A modern Bedouin desert camp.

A San hunter with traditional weapon.

DO MANY people live in the desert?

So named because they are largely deserted, the world's deserts have throughout history been very sparsely populated regions, inhabited only by small tribes of nomads.

But over the last hundred years or so the modern world has piled in, searching for valuable oil, gas, and minerals. Large cities have sprung up in the desert, bringing in power, water and air conditioning - from above it often looks like a vast alien spaceship has landed in the middle of nowhere.

The desert has now reclaimed Kolmanskop, a diamond-mining town in the Namib abandoned more than forty years ago.

THE SAN

Also known as Bushmen, the San are the oldest inhabitants of Southern Africa, living as nomadic hunter-gatherers in the Kalahari desert for more than twenty thousand years, well back into the Stone Age.

Traditionally wearing just a loincloth, they live in caves or simple thatched shelters made of twigs and branches. While the women gather plants, roots and nuts, the men hunt game with spears or bows and poisoned arrows.

The San are legendary animal trackers, and although small and slight they have extraordinary stamina, able to run for hours on end in the heat of the desert chasing prey such as antelope. The animal will usually succumb to exhaustion well before the San hunter.

Many of the San people were evicted from the Kalahari by the Government of Botswana in 2005, but the next year the tribespeople won a landmark case, which ruled they had the right to stay on their ancestral land.

Even so, only a small number of the San now live their traditional hunter-gatherer life in the desert.

COOL DESIGN

Desert peoples of hot regions are often the very opposite in build to the short, stocky Inuit (see Inuit Survival, page 60). The lean build of desert inhabitants gives them more surface area for their volume, helping them to lose heat and stay cool. Their bodies generally have little fat to keep heat in. Larger noses stop the air heating up further as it is breathed in.

Serious

THE AMAZING AMAZON

It's the greatest rainforest in the world with the greatest river in the world flowing through it, but it's only when you learn some of the amazing Amazon statistics that its huge significance really hits home:

THE FLOODED FOREST

One of the most remarkable facts about the Amazon region is that its appearance changes dramatically with the seasons. The water level of the Amazon river rises by as much as 15 m (50 ft) during the rainy season between November and May. Huge areas of forest are flooded and the maximum width of the river increases from 10 to 40 km (6 to 25 miles). Tributaries appear and islands disappear, so no map is ever entirely accurate.

Amazon

THE AMAZON RAINFOREST

Covers 6 percent of the earth's land surface

Makes up half of the world's remaining tropical rainforest

Spans eight countries, Bolivia, Peru, Ecuador, Colombia, Venezuela, Guyana, Suriname, and, most importantly, Brazil

A large area is destroyed every year by logging or farming

Contains more than one-third of all species of plants and animals in the world, many of them highly endangered

THE AMAZON RIVER

By far the world's biggest river in terms of amount of water flow, greater than the next eight largest rivers combined

Around 6,500 km (4,000 miles) in length, and in a long-running dispute with the Nile over which is the world's longest river (it depends on the definition of the start point)

Has its source high in the Peruvian Andes near the Pacific Ocean, but flows east all the way across South America to pour into the Atlantic at the Brazilian coast

Has over a thousand tributaries, some of them major rivers more than 1,500 km (1,000 miles) long

Home to the world's greatest variety of fish— around three thousand species—plus threatened animals like the pink river dolphin and Amazon manatee

The Amazon Basin

Iquitos in Relation to Amazon River and South America

0 — 500 miles
0 — 800 kms

The Amazon Basin is a huge low-lying area of South America, drained entirely by the Amazon River.

?– HOW DO YOU travel around the Amazon?

Apart from the tracks made by loggers there are almost no roads to be found in the Amazon, which means that traveling around this vast area is extremely difficult.

The Amazon and its tributaries have always been the "roads" of the forest, with canoes the traditional form of transport. Most communities are to be found by a river (with huts near the river built on stilts to cope with the huge rise and fall in river level each year).

The Amazon river itself is so wide and deep that oceangoing liners can travel all the way to the Peruvian river port of Iquitos, more than 3,000 km (2,000 miles) upriver.

Light aircraft have a very limited number of landing strips in the forest, and it can be quite unsettling flying for hours over the canopy in the knowledge that there is absolutely nowhere to land in an emergency. Float planes are also used, but again landing areas are limited. They have to find a long enough stretch of river without sharp bends, and be sure there are no logs or debris just below the surface.

As soon as you're away from a river it's walking only, which means the majority of the rainforest still remains unvisited. The Amazon covers an area similar to Western Europe, and is often flooded, swampy and impenetrable.

Many environmentalists are against more roads through the Amazon as they believe the few existing routes (like the Trans-Amazonian Highway) have led to an increase in rainforest destruction. But the Brazilian Government argues that controlled road-building is essential to help bring prosperity to the many poor people living on the fringes of the rainforest.

The flooded forest is home to a unique range of plants and animals, with river dolphins and manatees swimming among submerged trees. The swampy areas left as the waters recede are mosquito heaven, and as a result complete hell for humans.

The constantly changing landscape makes expedition planning tricky. Serious Amazon leaders took a canoe journey down a tributary when scouting for a training camp location, but when they returned just a week later with the young adventurers found the river completely impassable—the level had dropped by more than 2 m (7 ft), revealing huge logs that had been well below the surface but now blocked the route.

POVERTY AND AMAZON DESTRUCTION

Millions of Brazilians live in extreme poverty, and many have been encouraged to slash and burn the forest to farm on. Ironically, the rainforest soil is actually quite infertile and the poor farmers constantly have to move on, destroying ever more rainforest. Any global initiatives to stabilize the rainforest will need to take the farmers' needs into account.

Nevertheless, as in Borneo, corruption and big business still account for most of the destruction taking place, with illegal logging rampant and vast areas given over to commercial cattle ranching and agriculture.

The Serious Amazon Adventure

The starting-off point for the Serious Amazon expedition was the atmospheric Amazon river port of Iquitos in Peru. In the dense Amazon rainforest most local people rely on boats to travel any distance, and the young adventurers were no exception. For much of the trip the team members would use dug-out canoes, but to cover the 160 km (100 miles) from Iquitos to their rainforest training camp they had the luxury of an exhilarating ride up the Amazon in a powerboat, which whisked them to their remote base in just a few hours.

When hammering along at speed, the breeze is deceptively pleasant, but as soon as they pulled up to the riverbank in the heart of the rainforest the heat and humidity hit them full on.

For the first week, which consisted of training and acclimatization, their home was a basic thatched hut on stilts, with no running water or electricity. Just how basic things were was brought home when the expedition leader Ben Major cautioned the team that snakes and other creatures love to live in the thatch, and pointed out all the holes beneath the hut made by spiders.

Later that first evening his warnings were borne out as a huge tarantula was seen scurrying around in the rafters. Some of the team were rather spooked so early in the trip, so the leaders used a broom to persuade the hairy spider to leave the room.

Before the main expedition began, a gentle night learning to camp out in the rainforest was planned, but in the event it proved something of an expedition in its own right. The team were due

The adventurers traveled by powerboat up the Amazon before heading into a smaller tributary, the Yarapa river.

to paddle to the location in large dugout canoes, but the river levels had fallen dramatically since the expedition leaders checked out the route, and their way was blocked by logs which had previously been submerged.

It meant dragging the half-ton canoes overland and trekking through thick rainforest. By the time the adventurers arrived they were utterly exhausted, and they still had to put up their hammocks and bashas (see page 108).

After nightfall they had a frustrating time failing to light their campfire, they heard the scary sound of deadfall as a dead tree crashed to the ground nearby, and one of the team saw a snake near her sleeping area. All in all, another average day in the rainforest.

The challenging Extreme Amazon environmental missions involved two colorful, endangered creatures. They would be helping rare red uakari monkeys by building a massive breeding enclosure, but first they undertook a marathon canoe journey to help pink river dolphins. The aim was to rid 30 km (20 miles) of river of illegal fishing nets which trap the endangered mammals (see page 192).

Canoeing all day under a tropical sun in extreme humidity and air temperatures of more than 32°C (90°F) was debilitating, and team morale began to sink as they failed to find any fishing nets for two days.

To add to the stress, their last day on the river saw torrential downpours. It felt surprisingly cold and spirits were at a low, but there was a silver lining to the awful weather. Word was that the "jungle telegraph" had been warning the illegal fishermen the team was on its way. However, in the pouring rain the poachers had apparently let their guard down and put their nets back up.

With help from the local forest police, the Extreme Amazon adventurers finally removed three nets in all and completed their mission. It was ultimately little more than a token gesture in tackling the widespread problem, but important in helping raise awareness of the illegal plundering of the Amazon's natural resources.

The Amazon adventurers gather in an illegal net. The fine mesh nets are laid right across rivers, trapping everything from fish to river dolphins.

Their epic 30 km (20 mile) river journey now gave way to another epic task, the building of a 10 m (33 ft) square breeding enclosure for highly endangered red uakari monkeys in the middle of the rainforest. The huge enclosure would be made of brick and wire mesh, and the whole thing needed to be finished in just one week.

The young adventurers were spurred on by meeting the first two red uakari monkeys who would live in the enclosure, a male, Fran, and a female, Pepita. Both had been kept illegally as pets and rescued by a local charity.

In the tropical heat the work was incredibly tough, not least as the rainforest building site was full of bugs, from giant cockroaches to poisonous caterpillars. A reward for laying all three thousand bricks was a pause in building for an unbelievable once-in-a-lifetime treat, a visit to a threatened tribe, the Ashuar Indians, deep in the jungle.

With just days to go on the building project there was very bad news—one of the rare monkeys, Fran, had died. His funeral made the adventurers even more determined to complete the enclosure in his memory. In a moving opening ceremony the leader of the Ashuar tribe blessed the finished enclosure in traditional fashion, and Pepita appeared to take immediately to her new luxury home.

THE ASHUAR INDIANS

The Serious Amazon team paid a unique visit to one of the Amazon's most threatened tribes, the Ashuar Indians. They traveled deep into the rainforest in small, two person canoes to find the remote tribe. Cut off from modern life, it was like entering a different world.

The Ashuar are one of four branches of the feared Jivero tribespeople, best known for their

An Ashuar shaman blesses the Serious Amazon enclosure.

practice of shrinking human heads. Thankfully the tribe now lead a peaceful life, surviving as they always have on the rainforest around them.

But their simple way of life is under great threat, as logging destroys the forest around them and overfishing empties the rivers. As life gets tougher many have left the tribe to eke out an existence in "civilization," and there are just a few hundred pure Ashuar left.

For the young adventurers, taking part in traditions unchanged for generations was a deeply moving experience. (See also Amazon Tribes, page 208.)

The adventurers are given a traditional welcome (below) as they arrive at the Ashuar village.

EXPEDITION LOCATION

COLOMBIA

Puca Urco

Putumayo

Santa Clotilde

Napo

Negro Urco
Santa Rosa

San Felipe

Pebas

Francisco de Orellana
Huanana

Amazon (Amazonas)

P E R U

Sta Maria de Nanay
San Juan
Iquitos

Bellavista

Tamshiyacu

Omaguas

Tigre

Payorote

Puerto Franco
Nauta

Dolphin Corner

Yarapa

Marañón

Saquena

Ucayali

Bagazán

Pacaya Samiria National Reserve

Requena

Elvira

B R A Z I L

Yavari

0   50 miles

0   80 kms

73°

4°

COLOMBIA

area of map

Amazon

PERU

B R A Z I L

CHILE

ARGENTINA

Surrounded by dense rainforest, Iquitos, Peru's main river port, cannot be reached by road or rail.

The Serious Amazon team began their adventure by flying into Iquitos, Peru's main Amazon river port. With a population of 370,000, Iquitos is the largest city in the world that can't be accessed by road. It is completely surrounded by rainforest and can only be reached by boat or plane.

The city is just 130 km (80 miles) downstream from the start of the Amazon, where the mighty river forms from the Marañón and Ucayali rivers.

Serious Amazon was based a little way up the Yarapa river, the very first tributary of the Amazon, near an area known as Dolphin Corner, so-called because of the large number of pink river dolphins that gather there.

Amazon Wildlife

The range of Amazon wildlife is staggering. So much remains to be discovered and cataloged that it's impossible to put accurate figures on the huge diversity, but the Amazon is thought to contain over five hundred types of mammal, hundreds of reptile and bird species, thousands of types of fish, and millions of insect species. It's reckoned about one-third of all types of animal on the planet are found here; the key species below represent just a tiny selection (see also What Lurks Beneath, page 196).

JAGUAR

The threatened jaguar is the largest member of the cat family in the Americas, with most found in the Amazon. It looks similar to a leopard but is larger, up to 2 m (6 ft 6 in) in length and more well-built.

Hunting alone, the big cat is not a fussy eater. Prey range from capybaras and peccary to fish and birds, and they will even take anacondas and small crocodiles. Jaguars rarely attack humans unless threatened, and you would be extremely privileged to spot one.

Black jaguars are sometimes known as black panthers. In fact, a "panther" is not a specific type of animal, but a term used loosely to describe jaguars, pumas, and leopards.

The population of jaguars was devastated in the twentieth century by hunting for its coat, which is now generally banned. Current threats include loss of forest habitat and shooting by farmers as the jaguar is increasingly forced to attack cattle.

RED UAKARI MONKEY

Of all the monkeys in the Amazon, from howlers to spider monkeys, the red uakari (pronounced wuh-CAR-ee), is one of the rarest and least studied.

As the red uakari's habitat is destroyed and numbers drop, wildlife groups such as the Peruvian-based charity ISPTR (International Society for the Preservation of the Tropical Rainforest) are trying to persuade local people not to take the rare animals from the wild.

ISPTR rescues young uakaris taken illegally as pets, and asked Serious Amazon to build a large enclosure in the heart of the rainforest where the rescued monkeys could live and breed, before returning to the wild where possible.

This small monkey is about 50 cm (20 in) tall with a stubby tail too short to use for climbing. It has a striking bright red, hairless face, giving it a strangely human appearance.

Uakaris have traditionally been eaten by tribespeople, with the young often kept as pets in poor conditions.

PINK RIVER DOLPHIN

Also known as the Amazon river dolphin or boto, it's perhaps a little disappointing to find that this endearing, friendly creature is more often gray in color, although some individauls do indeed become pink with age.

This endangered mammal is the biggest of all river dolphins at up to 2.5 m (8 ft) in length, and is only found in the Amazon river and the Orinoco (which flows though Colombia and Venezuela).

The pink river dolphin has a highly developed sonar system which enables it to cope with the murky Amazon waters and swimming among the trees in flooded forests.

Threats include accidental trapping in fishing nets and the local tradition of using dolphin body parts as lucky charms.

TOUCAN

Found only in the Central American and Amazon region, there are about forty species of toucan, all notable for their enormous beaks which can be half as long as their bodies. Although the colorful beak looks unwieldy, it is in fact made of very light bone. Its function is unclear, perhaps helping the toucan eat large fruit or in taking eggs and chicks from other birds' nests.

MANATEE

The Amazonian manatee is one of three species of this endangered, slow-moving mammal. It's the only manatee species to live exclusively in freshwater, found solely in the waters of the Amazon and never straying out to sea.

Humans are the creature's main threat. Many manatees are drowned in fishing nets or killed by boat propellers.

-ⓘ-WHAT'S THE DIFFERENCE between river dolphins and ocean dolphins?

Of more than forty types of dolphin just four species are found in freshwater—the pink, Yangtze, Ganges, and La Plata river dolphins.

River dolphins don't perform the gymnastic leaps of their oceangoing cousins, and generally have a much more bulbous head with a long, narrow snout, which they use for searching for food on the riverbed.

The river dolphins are among the most endangered of all the world's dolphins, with the Yangtze river dolphin in China recently declared by conservationists to be extinct.

RECORD BREAKERS

The Amazon has many record-breaking species, including:

- Capybara—the world's largest rodent, which looks like a monster guinea pig. It's about the same size as a farmyard pig and often eaten.
- Giant otter—this highly endangered otter is the longest in the world, growing up to 1.8 m (6 ft). It can also sadly claim to be the rarest mammal in the Amazon, prized by hunters for its dense, velvety fur.
- Bird-eating spider—with a body that measures about 7.5 cm (3 in) and a leg span of around 30 cm (12 in), this is the world's largest spider. It eats insects and animals such as mice and small birds.
- Hyacinth macaw—this beautiful bird is the world's biggest parrot, at 1 m (40 in) in height. It's now endangered as it is unfortunately a highly sought-after pet, and is also hunted by tribespeople for its fine feathers.
- Arapaima—also known as the pirarucu, this is often cited as the world's largest freshwater fish, though larger catfish have been caught. Even so, the arapaima's vital statistics are extraordinary, sounding like a fisherman's tall tale—it can grow to 3 m (10 ft) in length and weigh around 200 kg (440 lbs).

THE SERIOUS AMAZON RIVER DOLPHIN PROJECT

One of the great problems facing the Amazon river system is illegal overfishing. Driven by demand in the big cities, gangs employ teams of fishermen to lay fine-mesh nets right across tributaries, plundering the river and depriving local people of a food source they've relied on for generations.

Both the size of the nets and the way they're laid is illegal as the nets catch everything in their path, including pink river dolphins, which may be trapped underwater and drown. The Serious Amazon team worked with Peruvian forest police and ISPTR to highlight the problem, clearing 30 km (20 miles) of river of illegal nets.

What Lurks Beneath

The reputation of many of the Amazon River's dangerous creatures is fearsome. In some cases it's fully deserved, but it may sometimes be more the stuff of myth and legend.

ANACONDA

Found only in South America, the giant anaconda is the world's largest snake, reaching over 10 m (33 ft) in length—though most are around half that size. Like its Asian cousin the reticulated python, the anaconda is a constrictor, killing its victim by squeezing till it suffocates (see Dangerous Creatures, page 82).

Active mainly at night, Anacondas lie in wait for their victims with just their eyes and nostrils above the water. They'll take anything from turtles to larger animals like deer and spectacled caimans, sinking their teeth into the neck before constricting them. They will often drag land-based prey into the water and drown them, before swallowing them whole.

CAN YOU swim in the Amazon?

If you listen to the more sensational descriptions of what lurks beneath the surface of the Amazon you'd never dip in a toe for fear of it being bitten off, but the truth is that some parts of the river at certain times of day are perfectly safe. Yes, there are piranha, anacondas, and crocodiles in some parts of the 6,500 km (4,000 mile) river, but local people have been bathing safely in the river and its tributaries for generations.

They know by bitter experience whether dangerous creatures inhabit their part of the river, along with the times and conditions to avoid. The expedition leader should make an assessment with help from local guides. In general, dusk and nighttime are much more of a problem.

In April 2007 a Slovenian swimmer named Martin Strel became the first person to swim the entire length of the Amazon. During his 66-day epic journey he successfully managed to avoid any attacks by the river's more deadly inhabitants.

There are endless gory tales of attacks on humans but this is in fact very rare. Anacondas are actually very wary of people and will usually slither silently away.

CAIMAN

Several species of caiman are found in the waters of the Amazon, including the endangered black caiman, the spectacled caiman, and a couple of smaller species.

Although often referred to as a type of crocodile, they are more accurately members of the crocodilian family (which includes caimans, alligators, and true crocodiles).

- The most dangerous is the black caiman, which may be more than 4.5 m (15 ft) in length. The population was decimated by hunting for its skin, and it is not found at all in many parts of the Amazon River.

An anaconda feeds on an ibis, having first drowned the bird.

?- DO ALL crocodiles eat humans?

Most big crocodiles and alligators are extremely dangerous. Although humans are not their first choice of food they will probably not turn you down if they are hungry. The power of their bite is phenomenal and once they have a firm grip it is unlikely they can be fought off, as they shake their victim from side to side inflicting terrible injuries.

The theory says a sharp punch to the snout may get them to release their grip, but it would be advisable never to have to put it to the test.

Smaller crocodile species are unlikely to try to eat a human, and will usually make themselves scarce rather than confront what they see as a larger predator.

- Spectacled caimans reach at most 2.5 m (8 ft) in length and are much more common. They get their name from a ridge of bone between their eyes which (supposedly) makes them look like they're wearing glasses. While potentially dangerous to humans they are much more likely to flee at the sound of people approaching.
- Cuvier's dwarf caiman is one of the world's smallest crocodiles, reaching only 1.5 m (5 ft) long with a heavily armored, bony skin.

PIRANHA

Images from the movies of schools of piranhas reducing a human to a skeleton in seconds have exaggerated the threat of this carnivorous fish.

Found exclusively in South America, there are about twenty species of piranha—of which only a few are dangerous to humans. Most infamous are red-bellied piranhas, which do occasionally take part in the classic feeding frenzy, stripping prey to the bone with their razor-sharp teeth.

Incidents involving people are, however, very rare as they prefer smaller prey and will usually only go for humans if starved. It's actually much more common for people to strip piranha to the bone as they are a very tasty fish eaten throughout the Amazon.

The Serious Amazon adventurers swam in a tributary where a much more innocuous type of piranha was found, receiving no more than tiny nips to the skin.

ELECTRIC EEL

Native to South America, electric eels can generate an electric charge of up to six hundred volts. The electric shock is used to stun prey and for self defense, and is generated by special organs in the eel's body (away from the head area). The charge will give humans a nasty shock but is unlikely to prove fatal.

One of the Serious Amazon adventurers with an electric eel captured by guides during a nighttime wildlife trip. The eel was subsequently released.

WHAT LURKS ABOVE

Going on expedition in the Amazon is a bit of a double whammy, as there are also all the usual jungle dangers away from the water, from mosquitoes to spiders to scorpions (see Dangerous Creatures, page 82). Among the more deadly creatures found in the Amazon rainforest:

- Poison arrow frog—also known as the poison dart frog, this tiny colorful frog is only up to 5 cm (2 in) long. However, it secretes one of the most toxic known poisons through its skin, so strong that a small drop can kill a large animal. The frog gets its name from the fact that the poison is used by local tribespeople on the tips of their arrows. There are many different species of poison arrow frog, some far more dangerous than others. Most have bright colorings to warn predators not to try to eat them. People should of course avoid touching them, as even brushing against the most toxic poison arrow frogs will result in severe skin irritation.

- The bushmaster and fer-de-lance are two of the Amazon's most deadly species of snake. Most common is the fer-de-lance (pictured below), which is a type of pit viper. It has very powerful venom and accounts for more deaths than any other animal in the Amazon (apart from the malaria-carrying mosquito). The bushmaster is one of the largest venomous snakes of all at 4 m (13 ft), and is much rarer than the fer-de-lance. Bites are rare but can be fatal without prompt action.

CANDIRU

This tiny, translucent South American fish is only about 2.5 cm (1 in) long, but has a rather gruesome reputation as a parasite that lives on the blood of other fishes or creatures, including humans.

It attaches itself by short spines, and unfortunately—grit your teeth—may lodge itself inside body parts including penises and vaginas. The candiru is then so difficult to extract that

victims may need an operation. Locals often wear tight-fitting underwear to protect themselves and also avoid peeing while in the water as this seems to help the candiru home in on its target.

Tales of candiru swimming up a stream of urine when people are peeing from the shore or from boats are almost certainly nonsense. That would be the equivalent of a human swimming up the Niagara Falls.

Emergency Survival

Being dumped in a jungle with nothing but the clothes you're wearing is the stuff of survival experts and military training. There are endless manuals showing the theory of how to survive using the riches of the rainforest around you—making natural shelters, drinking from vines, eating berries and bugs. It may even look quite fun but in reality it's extremely tough, even with serious training and experience.

Thankfully true emergency survival situations like this are very rare, encountered only in a disaster like a plane crash or most commonly if you get lost. Hopefully you will have your emergency belt kit filled with lifesaving provisions for just this scenario (see Essential Kit, page 14).

EMERGENCY SHELTERS

Building a shelter which can keep you dry in a tropical downpour is a lot harder than it may seem. A Serious Jungle survival training exercise had to be abandoned in the middle of the night during a rainstorm—the roof failed completely and as the water poured in the adventurers were in danger of developing hypothermia.

On the plus side it's worth remembering that there's very little wind in the rainforest so rain won't be blown in the side of a shelter. Check if there's a natural feature nearby to minimize the work. For example, a thick fallen log propped up on a bank could form part of the roof.

Local people have spent generations perfecting the techniques for weaving palm leaves or similar into watertight roofs, so if possible this is something to be practiced as part of expedition training. As with tiled or thatched roofs the principle is to overlap roofing materials so that the rain runs off (start with the lowest layer and work up). Thin branches are used to make a frame, and vines may be used to lash the frame together and tie the leaves on.

In an ideal world you would get off the ground to sleep, avoiding dangerous bugs and beasties, but in an emergency this is probably a carpentry job too far. So scrape the ground all around the shelter before you go to bed, to clear it of foliage and debris. Snakes and scorpions are less likely to cross open areas.

EDIBLE PLANTS

While the rainforest is undoubtedly a gigantic larder of edible plants and fruits, things once again are not that easy. Identifying what can safely be eaten is a job for the local expert, and you could all too easily make yourself very ill. There are many tales of folk who thought they knew their mushrooms, for example, and ended up poisoning themselves. So many different species look so similar that the golden rule has to be: if in doubt, go without.

WHAT'S THE KEY to emergency survival in the rainforest?

As with any emergency the most important thing of all is a positive mental attitude—the belief that you can and will survive. Put behind you the bad luck or stupidity that got you into the predicament in the first place. (Some of the most celebrated adventurers have done some very stupid things in their time.) Calmly take stock of the situation. Your belt kit contains enough food and water to keep you going for a good few hours, and you should also have the means to start a fire. Priorities are finding water and making a shelter, followed by fire and food.

The Serious Amazon team underwent emergency survival training, including finding water in vines and building shelters.

FINDING WATER

With iodine in the belt kit to purify water, the usual places—fast-flowing rivers and streams—should be tapped first (see page 102). If they are not available there are other sources, but as ever you need to know what you're doing. For example, some vines hold lots of drinkable water, but it's Sod's Law that other similar vines are actually poisonous—so you need a bit of specialist knowledge to identify which is which.

Probably the best alternative source is the rain itself. Simple collection systems can be rigged up to collect it more quickly, though even in the rainforest there can of course be long periods of no rain at all.

TRAPPING ANIMALS

It's tempting to think that in an emergency you will be able to build fiendishly clever traps and capture all sorts of delicious animals.

Unfortunately it's time for a reality check once more. The skill, time, and energy involved, coupled with the high chance of capturing nothing at all, make trapping animals a non-starter in a serious survival situation.

The river is, to coin a phrase, another kettle of fish and can be much more fruitful. There are many ways to trap fish, but perhaps the simplest is to improvise fish-hooks from pieces of metal (such as safety pins or needles) and leave them baited on a line crossing a river.

This beautifully made trap (right) uses some bait to tempt a small animal inside. When the prey walks through the cord, the stick is automatically pulled away and the trap falls.

Large palm leaves (left) have been made into a simple funnel to collect rainwater.

?–IS IT NECESSARY to eat bugs and creepy crawlies?

If you want to survive it may well be. Food is the body's fuel and without it you will quickly start to feel weak and cold. An emergency situation is not the time to be a fussy eater, and smaller creatures like insects are likely to be the easiest to get your hands on. While you will obviously need to eat quite a lot, some of the less savory jungle inhabitants like worms, grubs, termites, and ants are full of goodness.

The eight Serious Amazon adventurers roasted a tarantula on the fire and then (conveniently) had a leg each, sucking out the small amount of meat. It tasted a bit like crab.

If the "yuk" factor is getting the better of you, it's useful to remember that many of these creatures are delicacies to local people. Also, if you analyse what people eat back in "civilization" it's not actually that different. Think of prawns or snails or even, dare one say, a cow's bottom.

Cooking in boiling water may help them to be more palatable and will also kill parasites.

In anything but an emergency situation take advice from a local guide as to what is safe to eat. As a general rule, brightly colored creatures contain toxins and anything that smells bad is not good.

A rainforest feast, including snails and a small caiman.

Designed to catch animals the size of a small monkey (demonstrated here by one of the Serious Amazon adventurers), this trap needs someone to monitor it constantly. Hidden nearby, that person releases the rope holding up the cage the moment an animal gets inside.

Dugout Canoes

Locals who've been canoeing down the river since before they could walk make it seem effortless, but paddling a dugout canoe for hours on end is far harder than it looks. On the plus side most dugout canoes are a lot safer than they may appear. The four-person traditional canoes used by Serious Amazon were hollowed-out tree trunks weighing more than half a ton and took a lot of skill to maneuver.

CANOE SAFETY

Before a long canoe trip it's important to practice "man-overboard" and capsize drills. First, though, you must choose a section of river deemed safe by leaders and local guides.

Capsize drill

Once in the water, your chief priority is getting the canoe back in action. All your possessions should be left and collected later, which is why it's so important that backpacks are fully waterproofed (see page 15).

To right the canoe, the crew need to reach over to the far side and use their weight to pull it back over. After bailing a little water out, one of the team can clamber aboard to get out the remainder. A paddle is useful for scooping it out.

While it is usually recommended that life jackets are worn at all times when on water, Serious Amazon weighed up the risks and decided against wearing them for this particular expedition. The leaders felt that wearing the bulky jackets while paddling in high humidity under the tropical sun would lead to an unacceptably high chance of heat exhaustion.

Instead each crew member was attached by cord to a life jacket which sat next to them in the canoe in case of emergency. If the canoe capsized the life jacket would end up next to the adventurer in the water.

To gain confidence in the stability of their canoes, the Serious Amazon adventurers stand on the sides rocking from side to side.

?—ARE DUGOUT CANOES stable?

The first time you get in one you'll probably feel incredibly unstable. Dugout canoes seem very low in the water and appear to rock precariously, tipping almost to the water line. But as you spend more time paddling about you find it's actually really hard to tip them far enough to capsize. These are designs that have been passed down the generations, so it figures that they must be effective to have stood the test of time.

Serious Amazon used the Ashuar Indians' own two-person dugout canoes to reach the tribe's remote village. There are accounts of Ashuar children as young as eight making their first canoe.

One of the young adventurers cheerfully leaps into the water as part of a "man-overboard" drill.

MAKING DUGOUT CANOES

It's thought dugout canoes are among the first watercraft ever built. Crafting them from tree trunks is not to be underestimated. Hollowing out and carving solid logs is tricky enough even with modern tools like chainsaws, and the early canoes would have been made using the most primitive stone axes and scrapers (controlled burning of the wood was sometimes used to make it easier to hollow out the logs).

The exact style of the craft is critical to a canoe's performance, with the knowledge and skills passed on from generation to generation. Often the construction involves heating and stretching the hull to make the desired shape. This is truly no mean feat with few tools available.

Crossing Rivers

When hiking though the jungle, you will almost inevitably come to a river you need to cross. This is one of the most dangerous activities of all, and must never be undertaken lightly. Possible dangerous creatures are one thing (and advice will need to be taken from local guides as to whether the river's safe), but the real hazard is the water itself. River currents can be very deceptive and you may quickly find yourself being swept away, especially if weighed down by kit and clothing.

BEFORE YOU BEGIN

- Always ask yourself whether you really need to cross the river at all. Is there an alternative?
- Avoid any particularly fast-flowing areas. Rocks underneath the surface may form mini-rapids.
- Look for sandbanks or other easy crossing points. In the Amazon this won't include bridges. Because of the huge seasonal variation in the width of the river there aren't any.

- Check there are easy exit points on the opposite bank, bearing in mind that depending on the current you may be coming out a fair way downstream.
- Ensure the river has been given the all-clear for dangerous creatures by local guides.
- Check you have completely waterproofed your backpack (see page 15).

An expedition leader will go first to check out the depth of the river and the currents. A stick may be used for balance and to check the depth ahead. A common safety technique is to hold onto a rope anchored back on shore by two others standing some distance apart, who can always haul the leader back in case of difficulty. Assuming the river is crossable, this rope can then be anchored at the other side to help with the crossing.

CROSSING TECHNIQUES

a) Shallow enough to wade across

Make sure your backpack is loose enough to come off easily if you fall and get swept away, otherwise it may drag you under. It's advisable to use only one shoulder strap. If the river is fast-flowing and you don't have a rope, form a triangle of people with arms over each other's shoulders to avoid being swept away. Include one of the strongest members of the team in each group.

b) Swimming across

Your backpack can be used as a float by trapping lots of air in the main waterproof liner before resealing. The safety rope may be slung at water level, or high enough to allow a smaller rope to be attached by climbing clip and hang down. (Known as a cowstail, this can then move along the tensioned line as you swim.)

Either way, it'll be tiring holding on while kicking out with boots on. Take it steadily and expect progress to be slow, otherwise you could be completely exhausted by the time you get to the middle of the river.

BACKPACK RAFT

The Serious Amazon team practiced a possible technique for helping an injured colleague to cross a river, tying all their inflated backpacks together to make a raft. In an emergency the casualty could then rest on top while the other team members propel the raft across the river.

?-SHOULD YOU keep your boots on when swimming across a river?

There's no doubt that heavy boots make the going tougher, but on balance they are still to be recommended. You will have to wade in and out without knowing where you're putting your feet, and you could step on either a sharp rock or a variety of creatures who might not be pleased and understandably react by trying to bite. Boots will also help you keep your footing on slippery banks.

Amazon Tribes

It's common to hear the way of life of native peoples described as "primitive" compared to our lifestyle in "civilization." There's no doubt it's a far simpler, more basic existence, and we certainly have incredible comfort, convenience and luxury in the modern world. But by immersing ourselves constantly in such amazingly sophisticated devices as TVs, computers, and mobile phones, we are in great danger of losing touch with the natural world.

Tribespeople have an incredible depth of knowledge about how to live in harmony with nature, in environments that modern urban people find incredibly tough. They are the last link with our roots, and if they disappear, a wealth of human wisdom will disappear with them.

TRIBES UNDER THREAT

Before first contact with Europeans around five hundred years ago, it's estimated there were more than a thousand different Amazon tribes with a total population of well over two million. But as the world population has mushroomed, the local Amazon peoples have become ever more endangered. It's thought total numbers have now fallen to fewer than four hundred thousand—the population of a small town in the UK—spread across about two hundred and fifty tribes (who speak almost two hundred different languages).

The assault on their way of life by the "civilized" world over the past few centuries is shameful—stealing their land, killing those who resisted, taking people into slavery, cutting down the forest, polluting the rivers, and all the time exposing tribes to Western diseases, such as measles and chicken pox to which they had no resistance.

Brazil has now protected a total of 1,000,000 sq km (400,000 sq miles) of territory for native peoples, though policing this against illegal loggers is quite another matter.

The Kayapo have been one of the few tribes to successfully campaign for their rights on a world stage. With help from the rock star Sting they have stopped logging and mining on their land, and prevented a huge dam project from going ahead.

TRIBAL KNOWLEDGE

Native peoples draw on thousands of years of experience of living in the rainforest and their knowledge of plants and animals is unparalleled—relying on nature for their very existence.

Until recently, many believed the healers in the tribe, often known as shamans, operated at a purely spiritual level (put less politely that it was all "mumbo-jumbo"). Now it's recognized that they have invaluable insights into cures for all sorts of diseases, and scientists from drug companies are working closely with them to tap into their expertise. There are notorious examples of tribes being hoodwinked into giving away their knowledge, but there is now pressure to reward them fairly.

VISITING TRIBES

There is a great ethical debate about whether it's right to visit tribes, especially those which live a fairly separate existence. It crosses over into the more fundamental question of indigenous people integrating into the modern world. It is difficult to achieve a balance between the benefits of modern comforts and medicine, and the loss of tradition and harmony with nature.

Many would argue that it should be the tribe's own decision, as long as they fully understand the consequences. There are lots of reputable tour groups with organized trips to fairly integrated tribes, though the tribal displays will often be put on just for tourists and are no longer practiced for real.

The adventurers try out blowpipes and bows and arrows during their visit to the endangered Ashuar tribe. The Ashuar were happy to be visited by Serious Amazon in order to highlight their struggle for survival.

-?-ARE THERE any tribes left who've had no contact with the outside world?

This appears to be one of those Catch-22 questions—if we know about them doesn't it follow that they've had contact with "civilization?" Well, not necessarily. There are several tribes who definitely seem to know about the outside world but want no contact with it, attacking or even killing anyone who strays too close to their territory. From these incidents—and tapping into the knowledge of tribes who have made contact—it's possible to build up a rough picture. The Brazilian native people's agency FUNAI knows for sure of around twenty uncontacted tribes, and estimates the total

Like many tribes the Ashuar wear a mixture of traditional and modern Western clothes.

?– DO head-shrinkers and cannibals still exist?

Most of these practices have now died out, though some of the tribes who carried them out do still exist. For example, the Wari of Brazil who had a reputation for cannibalism, and the head-shrinking Jivero Indians of Peru (The Ashuar visited by Serious Amazon—see page 188—are a subgroup of the Jivero).

Like many tribes they were fierce defenders of their territory from neighboring peoples, and the gruesome customs were traditional ways of dealing with their enemies. Both tribes are now generally peaceful, so no longer indulge.

There are, however, still some tribes who would not think twice about firing poison-tipped arrows at unwelcome guests, and it's not known which traditions are continued by the tribes who haven't made contact with the outside world.

Watching footage of themselves was a first for these tribespeople.

INDEX Entries in *italics* denote photographs

PICTURE CREDITS